The Teacup Ministry and Other Stories

The Teacup Ministry & Other Stories

Rhoda H. Halperin

Subtle Boundaries of Class

University of Texas Press   Austin

First edition, 2001

Requests for permission to reproduce material from this work
should be sent to Permissions, University of Texas Press,
Box 7819, Austin, TX 78713-7819.

∞ The paper used in this book meets the minimum requirements
of ANSI/NISO Z39.48-1992 (R1997) (Permanence of Paper).

LIBRARY OF CONGRESS CATALOGING-IN-PUBLICATION DATA

Halperin, Rhoda H.
    The teacup ministry and other stories : subtle boundaries of
class / Rhoda H. Halperin.—1st ed.
        p.   cm.

    ISBN: 978-0-292-73143-1

    1. Working class—New Jersey—Case studies.   I. Title.
HD8083.N4 H35 2000
305.5'62'09749—dc21   00-044353

*To SMH, whose untimely death inspired this book,
and to SWH for remaining positive.*

Contents

Contents

Acknowledgments

Gail, Sal, Gloria, and Phil put their souls into family and community. Ruth, Eileen, Dorothy, John, and Margaret do the same. They are the spirits behind this book. Many others took great care and attention to provide helpful comments: The Hirschfeld family, Jimmy, Janet, Jennie, and especially Julie, Kathryn Borman, Kathleen DelMonte, Theresa May, Sue Eck, John Schafer. Judith and Alethea Marti. Ruth Jones, Elizabeth Royalty, and Barbara Stoll. Talks with Barry Isaac and Ken Kensinger helped formulate the major concepts. Michael Halperin read these stories with great interest and with enthusiastic and helpful comments. Sam provided inspiration.

Sophia met Solomon in the military—or a military branch of sorts. It was called the signal corps—electronics and radio, the high tech of the 1940s, where those with more brains than muscles could contribute to the war against fascism. A certain prestige attached to being selected for this special unit, a bit like the "smart camps" for kids with high IQs and computer skills but little interest in sports. He was her supervisor, or rather, the supervisor of a group of women workers contributing to the war effort. They tested equipment before it was sent overseas. To this day, Sophia protests that she thought Solomon was interested in her best friend, who sat to her left on the assembly line. Her friend, a petite, dark, striking woman, had won numerous beauty contests—so many, in fact, that Sophia thought herself ugly and large by comparison. You see, Solomon was only five feet two inches.

Two opposites they were, much like the poles of the complicated electrical systems they worked on. She had a bright complexion—blushing rosy cheeks and thick, light-brown curly hair that she tried to control with tortoise-shell combs. In grade school her teachers demanded that she "wipe that rouge off her face." Of course, she was embarrassed. "But it's natural," she'd protest meekly.

He was dark. Except for penetratingly blue eyes, he had black hair and sallow skin. When he had been in the sun he could pass for African American, and he was proud of that fact. It linked him to his childhood in the ghetto and it emphasized his natural sympathy for all humans, "regardless of race, creed, or color." He was fond of this phrase.

She was always moving—practicing modern dance as a young mother, tennis, walking, swimming—active and talkative, positive and upbeat. Her high energy seemed forced at times, as though she had to keep moving until she was exhausted, to avoid slothfulness, her version of laziness, or just thinking too much. For Sophia, actions spoke louder than words. She was never nervous, although she struggled for a sense of power and control that she tried to keep under the surface.

He was contemplative, sedentary, and moody. While he would talk incessantly in a charming way in his manic phases, he usually preferred to be alone with the newspaper or a good book. In his depressions he slept.

Sophia and Solomon were both the children of Eastern European immigrant parents who came to the United States as poor refugees. They struggled to make ends meet. Her parents owned a mom-and-pop grocery in Brooklyn. They worked long hours, especially Sophia's mother, who was also a domestic wizard: cooking, sewing, she could make anything, even after a hard day's work. When Sophia was a little girl, they'd send her to the bank on the subway with the daily cash deposit tucked into her clothing. A hat pin was her weapon and a hot sweet potato her solace and warmth. Sophia had to fight with her gambler father to go to college. He wanted her to work in the store. Luckily, her hardworking mother supported her higher education at the public, urban university. At the time it was the only coed institution in the City College system. She didn't want to go to Hunter College, which was all girls. (At that time, college girls were called girls, not women.)

Right after Sophia married Solomon, her mother died suddenly at the age of forty-eight. "She worked herself to death." Sophia always spoke of her mother with great admiration and sadness. Not only did she work full time, she also made beautiful clothes for Sophia, cooked and baked like a professional, and fermented her own cherries in a large vat on the fire escape.

Cherry vishniak, they used to call it. Sophia remembers tasting the deliciously sweet liqueur. The conventional wisdom may have attributed her death to overwork, but, more likely, she suffered a massive stroke or heart attack. They didn't know how to control high blood pressure then.

Solomon's father also died young. Solomon became the caretaker of his Philadelphia family at sixteen, when his father, a wallpaper hanger trained in Europe in classical violin, died of lip cancer. The money set aside for Solomon's medical education went instead for his father's cancer treatments, or so the story goes. They were poor, but cultured. Solomon's mother, Rose, a tiny woman with thinning black hair, was always reading—history, Russian novels, and newspapers in Russian, a language she refused to speak to anyone outside of her generation. Russian was, after all, "un-American." She attributed her near baldness to her long girlhood braids pulling on her scalp. Before 1920, she had worked on the assembly line in the now infamous Triangle Shirtwaist Factory, the one in which so many women workers had been killed in a horrible fire. She didn't like to talk about it, and the term *posttraumatic stress* had not been invented yet.

In the 1930s, Solomon and his younger brother, Martin, worked their way through college playing summers in their own band in bars in coastal towns and islands off the East Coast, such as Winston, Atlantic City, and towns further north—Solomon on piano, Martin on sax and clarinet. Solomon chose to study liberal arts and electronics at the local university, even though he had been accepted to the prestigious Curtis Institute of Music. The hours and whole days of practicing had paid off, but he wanted to branch out and get away from the endless drills and scales. He had also joined the Communist Party, a legacy he inherited from his radical, European father. Martin, who was much more carefree than Solomon, became a hard-living musician—corporate New York music executive by day, big-band sax player by night. His thirties found him still a confirmed bachelor, which in those days equaled a rejection of the institution of marriage. Finally, he married in his early forties, but divorced only ten years later. As a hobby, he wrote trashy novels and short stories, which, of course, he did under a pseudonym. Sophia was fond of quoting this fact. Whenever she talked about him, a distinct note of puritanism came into her voice. After work he dressed like a bum, so as not to get mugged on the streets late at night. His torn jackets and raggedy pants were part of a survival strategy, but they did not protect him from the pulmonary embolism that killed him at the age of sixty. Solomon never recovered from the death of Martin. His depressions got longer and deeper; anger often consumed him.

Before he met Sophia, Solomon had been engaged to "a Bryn Mawr girl," diamond engagement ring and all. As a private women's college in the East, Bryn Mawr was noted for its high academic standards, high tuition, and high level of elitism and snobbery. Sophia often repeated the mythical family story in which Solomon's mother, Rose, prepared an elaborate dinner for his fiancée's family. She polished silver, cooked all of her best dishes, and worried over the house, the food, and the table settings. After all of her efforts, the "Bryn Mawr girl's" family criticized Rose for failing to place the silverware exactly one inch from the edge of the table. Of course her Main Line family disapproved of Solomon's modest beginnings; he knew that in the abstract. Now it became real to him in a most painful way. They didn't care about his musical talents or his high academic standing. His sensitivity and good nature didn't matter to them. Solomon moped and brooded. Then he went off alone to the ocean, where he sat in a motel room for three days. When he came back, he announced the end of his engagement. But she never gave back the expensive ring.

Sophia took some pleasure in telling and retelling this story, especially the parts about the misplaced silverware and the expensive diamond ring. In a peculiar way, Sophia showed jealousy toward the defunct relationship, an odd combination of class competition and emotional warfare. When Sophia was angry at Solomon, she would tell him he should have married his "Bryn Mawr girl."

In the late 1940s, Solomon, his mother, and his brother moved from the slums of North Philadelphia to a row house on the city's periphery. As the oldest son, Solomon became the head of the household. He took financial responsibility for his mother and brother. The 13th Street house, as they called it, was spacious, with living room, dining room, and kitchen on the first floor and three bedrooms upstairs. It even had a full basement and garage. Sophia and Solomon lived there for the first seven years of their married life. The misery in Sophia's voice could be heard every time she mentioned 13th Street. "A hole in the wall is better than a palace, if it's yours and yours alone. Never live in someone else's house," she'd repeat over and over again. It became a litany. They later moved to the suburbs.

Just after Solomon died, almost twenty years after Martin's death, Solomon's children received a phone call from the adult child of Frances, Solomon and Martin's half brother, son of their father, Henry, from his first marriage. It seems that Henry's first wife had died giving birth to Frances, who was then adopted by his mother's sister and her husband in California. This explained his different last name and, in part, his absence from the lives of Solomon and Martin. Lauren, Solomon's daughter, had always wondered how her grandfather had lived without seeing his firstborn son for so many years. She never had a chance to ask him, though, since he died before she was born.

Ironically, perhaps, Frances, Solomon, and Martin turned out to be a lot alike. They were all rather bad at business. Solomon and Frances were just too nice and sensitive to be good businessmen. They loved music and were accomplished musicians. With the exception of Martin, whose daughter has been lost to the family with a drug problem connected to a bitter divorce, they produced professional children with nontraditional careers. They each in their own unique way remember where they came from. The children seek links to people who remind them of family class memories.

All three of Frances's children are psychotherapists working with diverse clients in Los Angeles and Phoenix. Solomon's son, Alan, is a public defender, and his daughter, Lauren, is a pediatrician specializing in diseases of children in medically underserved areas—urban communities and third world villages.

Class lines can divide; they can also be connected and realigned if you do not forget where you came from.

PART

Crossing Class Boundaries

I

Prologue

People from different life circumstances come together in moments of intensity and crisis.

The story "Beach Badges" recounts tensions developing between people of different classes when working-class people seem to trespass on elite spaces, in this case a coastal summer resort community on the East Coast. The tensions in this East Coast story directly parallel those between working-class East Enders and the power elite of a midwestern city. Developers and land bankers have always regarded working-class East Enders as invaders of elite riverfront property, even though the previously undesirable river bottoms have been home to East Enders for seven generations. When, for example, developers say that illiterate hillbillies have no right to views of the river, they are simply saying in a very blatant and blunt fashion, what the older woman in "Beach Badges" says much less directly. Assertions of class prerogatives come in many forms. (See "City Lines" in Part II and "Rehab" in Part III.)

In "Beach Badges," seemingly minute incidents, but nonetheless common, everyday ones, mark class and power. The events described mirror many other "class events" and class interactions. The public spaces in "Beach Badges" resemble the more formal public spaces one encounters in cities. Somehow, though, the casual, luxurious resort atmosphere allows for even more insidious power dynamics than those that play out in the formal contexts of city and local government.

Subtle class differences are not obvious in systems that are structured as polar oppositions: rich and poor, educated and uneducated, powerful and powerless. In "Beach Badges," a "piney" (a local term used as a stereotype for people who live in the remote pinelands) is different from a fisherman, although both have working-class and negative referents. Fishermen are familiar; pineys are unknown and therefore exotic and dangerous. In the Midwest, "river rats" have a specific place identification with the Ohio River, which is not only a source of livelihood, but a spiritual and aesthetic power. East Enders proudly refer to themselves as river rats. "Hillbilly" does not carry such positive associations; it is much closer to "piney."

People of different social classes are assumed to occupy their own social spaces. In "Beach Badges," would Gina, from the working-class mainland, and her family have ventured to the island's public, but nonetheless uppity beach without being accompanied by an old friend and longtime island resident at the height of the summer season? Some people easily cross class boundaries; others do not.

The fragility of steady work, the seasonality of it, and the fact that people are not self-defined by a single occupation are features in these stories as well. The strenuousness and managerial skill required by Gina to maintain a business that confers autonomy and a sense of independence come through in "Beach Badges," but these skills and talents must be understood in the context of multiple livelihood strategies that, historically, have been part of survival for working-class people. A single job cannot be relied upon to secure livelihood.

The season changes in "A Partridge in a Pear Tree," which is a story of class tensions mitigated by holiday gaiety. Gina's charm and skill, as well as her sensitivity to people, bring out the joy of celebration. Lauren ventures into foreign class territory. At the same time, the intimacy of the moment enables Monica, an elegant, working-class elder, to express to Lauren a part of her family's history of interclass relationships and class tensions. Here we see island-mainland tensions reflecting class tensions;

at the same time, we see the many important linkages between island and mainland people.

"Sudden Death" is the actual recounting of a death and its aftermath. The story is about sensitivity and insensitivity on the part of people of different social classes in a time of crisis. The unconditional caring demonstrated by the long-standing community members contrasts with the insensitivity and selfishness of the widow's elite summer friends.

Class generosity and spirituality are themes in "The Teacup Ministry," which explores the sensitivities that come with "being there" to help in a time of crisis. Here working-class people and elites switch places, at least temporarily. Religious lines are crossed as well. The fragility of class status and of a person's class position are accompanied by cycles of class positioning in the progression of the generations.

The temporary qualities as well as the permanent features of class positioning are reflected in "City House." Mark, a second-generation ophthalmologist, still ministers to the working class, just as his father did. Class mobility for people who had been working-class immigrants is another theme. The city house is a marker of class status, but a fragile one because its value declines with the encroachment of the city. In some contexts the city confers status and power; in others the proximity of the city signals decline.

Beach Badges

"The Island," as the locals call it, has always had a certain separateness to it. It's not just the six miles of bay sitting between the island and the mainland. From the island on a clear day you can see the vague outlines of buildings in the mainland towns of Breckenridge, Winston, and Morgantown, but most of the time the fog and mist hide the mainland's borders. Except for the threatening-looking electric power plant that serves as a beacon for boats making their passage through the inland waterway, these towns are invisible to the island's summer people, for whom the mainland remains mysterious and dangerous. Mainlanders, on the other hand, often know the island intimately, having worked there during the busy summer season, or lived there at one time or another.

The new causeway that now connects the mainland to the island is gigantic, a span of concrete and metal that is high enough for the tallest mast to pass under with ease. In the 1950s, before the causeway was built, a rickety old wooden bridge hovered close to the water. A troll-like man sat in a little house and worked the drawbridge. He seemed to crank it up and down by hand, slowly and deliberately. Riding over the bumps on that old bridge felt natural, connected to the water and the land, like being in a boat crossing the bay. People still talk about that old bridge. Sometimes the water was so high it covered the hubcaps, but the cars trudged onto the island anyway. The new causeway is intimidating and uncomfortable, with harsh lights built into the railings that burn your eyes at night. Cars stream over it, creating a strobelike effect, suspended in midair. When the northeasters blow in winter, school has to be canceled because it is too dangerous for the yellow buses to cross the causeway. It's a bridge that people hesitate to cross—islanders and mainlanders alike—unless, of course, there is a compelling reason to do so.

The island itself is a big sandbar, eighteen miles long and, at its widest, only a few blocks. Sparse vegetation—low cedars and bayberry bushes—cluster now on the few empty lots. They used to grow in profusion but gradually have been replaced by manicured flower gardens. In the nineteenth and most of the twentieth century, the island belonged to the fishermen who cast their nets out into the ocean or took boats out to sea. It was a precarious life, but one in which the local community, for most of the year, was left alone to claim the island. The island is still a beautiful, peaceful place, but it is being taken over by "summer people" from the cities. Oceanfront homes, most used only on summer weekends, sell for millions of dollars, and in some areas threatening signs with warnings like "No beach access, owners and guests only" forbid outsiders to trespass. Some of these "homes" look like hotels, they are so big and ornate, with turrets, marble floors, and swimming pools. Modest, humble dwellings are called "tear-downs," meaning that the person who buys the property should tear down the original old house and build a new, large one.

Seasoned locals make disparaging remarks about outsiders and their habits. The longtime owner of the gas station is a man in his seventies who, in his younger days, would jump in a boat or a tow truck to rescue anyone in need. Now he proudly points to his son, who has taken over most of the work. "These people stand in line in their cars to get here, they stand in line for their rolls and newspapers on Saturday and Sunday morning, and they stand in line again to get off the island. I like the month of February best. There is no standing in line."

In the 1950s I heard people talk about "the pineys," unusual folk living in the dense mainland pine forests. They were said to be "different." Pineys were supposed to be scary for their disorganized lives and their potential for violence. There was talk about pineys sitting on porches with shotguns to keep outsiders out of the pinelands. Piney children were said to go without shoes in winter and live in houses and trailers without heat and electricity, eating deer and squirrels with the few teeth remaining in their mouths. I never saw any houses or people in the pine woods though, as we drove east on the two-lane highway toward the ocean. Only produce stands with names like Carrot Top and Greensleeves Market broke the monotony of endless pine trees. I knew, even then, that "piney" was not a good word.

I knew also, somehow, that "piney" glossed differently from "fisherman" or "farmer." A large community of Norwegian immigrants had settled on the island in the town just north of ours. Most of the men worked as commercial fishermen—one of the most dangerous occupations in the industrialized world. The captains and their crews lived with their extended families in the community. In summer, the women worked in the vacation homes or in the shops and restaurants open only from Memorial Day to Labor Day. In winter they devoted themselves to raising children, worrying about their husbands at sea, and taking care of their extended families. Some of the elders went back to Norway to retire; others stayed. I learned some Norwegian words from our neighbor, Old Man Hakensen, as everyone called him, just before he died. His son and daughter-in-law took good care of him. He had a special warmth for children and would often spend hours telling stories of his childhood in Norway. *Bestapappa* meant grandfather, and he somehow filled in for the grandfathers I never knew.

What remains of the Norwegian community is a tourist area of rustic, tiny shacks called Viking Village. Gift shops, flower stands, and antique stores have names like "Little Scandinavia." The traditional intricately patterned, thick, woolen sweaters hang from the rafters, but they have little appeal in the dog days of summer. They seem hollow, as though in need of bodies to fill their limp torsos and sleeves.

Timmy Gunnerson, Old Man Hakensen's nephew, his wife, Gretchen, and his family lived on our street. He was a quiet man and kept mostly to himself. Gretchen talked to everyone in the neighborhood, on the street, and on the beach. Her smile and energy seemed limitless. When she did sit down, she always had a needle and thread in her hand. Their three children swam in the ocean with us, and as the summer progressed, their already blond hair turned white as they rode the waves for hours every day.

Each week during the summer, Earl, Gretchen's father, a "truck farmer" from the inland farm country, brought all of us fruits and vegetables at far below market rate: huge bunches of Swiss chard, tomatoes, melons of all sorts, and freshly picked corn. Some of it he grew himself; the rest he bought from wholesalers. He even husked the corn and put the ears in plastic bags with twist ties. (This was before zip-lock bags were invented.) He delivered fruits and vegetables to other people too, many of whom were fishermen like Timmy. Earl and Timmy had built their island house board by board. They had a good relationship for in-laws. Earl was proud of the house and his family on the coast. He could do anything with his hands. When Timmy caught a surplus of fish, he gave his neighbors some. He never let anyone pay. He was a very generous man—too generous, I often thought. Timmy and his family clearly were not "pineys," but their year-round life on the island was not easy. Gretchen cleaned houses to bring in extra money. "Piney" was always a puzzling term, something I always wondered about, something that was taboo to ask about. I knew, though, that for both pineys and fishermen, life could be very tough.

My parents used to go to Midnight Bob's with Earl and his "ladyfriend," Nellie, after they finished making their vegetable rounds. It's a silver-sided diner with round stools, a Formica counter, and tough but kindly waitresses who remember how you take your coffee. Earl, a very large, balding man, loved lots of good, wholesome food, and so did Nellie. She was a small, dark-haired, prim-and-proper-looking woman, always at Earl's side. They were definitely a couple. They also loved to talk. Nellie said little but seemed to take everything Earl said with great seriousness. She had a rather ambiguous position in the family and the community. She was neither Gretchen's mother nor Earl's wife but simply his "ladyfriend." She was often the subject of local gossip.

I never thought much about these lunches except that they would always rave about the rice pudding. The two couples seemed at ease with one another, but come to think of it, none of my parents' friends ever went along. I wondered about this too. How could it be that my childhood was somehow caught between the worlds of city and country, between people who had experienced the dangers of the sea and the vagaries of crop failures and people who thought food originated in supermarkets and that all one needed was the cash to purchase it?

In the late 1970s, Timmy and Gretchen moved their still young family to Florida, where the fishing was better and the weather less harsh. Large, commercial companies were beginning to take over the fishing dock where Timmy kept his boat. For a few summers after the family left, Earl and his ladyfriend continued to load their van with vegetables, distribute them among friends, and spend a day visiting or sitting on the beach. Then one day a local official asked for their vendors' license. Having none, they barely endured fingerprinting at the police station. They never returned.

Beach badges are required now on the island—seasonal, weekly, daily. They are small, quarter-sized plastic octagons with the year and the season written on the front and a strong, thick pin on the back. People pin them to everything—chairs, towels, backpacks. Twenty dollars for the season; five for a week. They're cheaper than going to the movies—admission tickets to the beach. Anyone can buy them simply by going to one of many municipal offices that sit prominently in the midst of these seashore communities. We didn't have beach badges when I was a kid; like zip-lock bags, they hadn't been invented yet.

It's a sunny Friday near the end of August 1997. Gina, self-defined local and my girlhood friend who lives in the mainland town of Breckenridge, calls to ask about borrowing beach badges.

Originally, Gina's family came from industrial northern New Jersey. They spent summers on the older, southern end of the island, which, historically, has always been densely populated, and, thus, less expensive than the northern end. Gina and I met as teenagers while working at the Dairy Queen. About fifteen years ago, Gina's family moved from "up north" to live permanently in the mainland rural town of Breckenridge. They thought it would be a better (safer) environment for raising kids and they were willing to travel north to work.

Gina's daughter, Sue, thirty-three, is visiting from rural Tennessee with her husband, Will. Will's originally from the East Coast, but his family moved to Tennessee when he was two years old. He's got a paunch, a blond ponytail, tattoos on his upper arms, and a farmer's tan, complete with a white ring around his ankles where his clearly short socks have been. Will says hello to me politely, but very tentatively as Gina pulls up in her big white boat of a car. He is very guarded even after Gina jumps out and gives me one of her bear hugs.

"Tell me again where the street is with the nice beach—you know—the one we went to a few weeks ago," queries Gina. "Or, do you want to go with us? There's plenty of room in the car."
I think a minute. Why not? It's a beautiful day. I've been cooking for what seems like an eternity.

I decide to take my car. We head north to 60th Street, the first public beach access road for several miles. It's the same place where the blond towheads had ridden the waves years ago. I point to a space for Gina to use and proceed up the house-lined street. Gina pulls into the space and then quickly out of it. She makes a U-turn into a spot across the street. I wonder what happened to Gina's first, perfectly legal parking space. As we proceed over the dunes, Gina confides that the people with the house just back from her parking space told her they were expecting company and that she should not park there.

"What!?" I exclaim to myself. "It's a public street. They have no right to shoo her away. Would they have said that to a person driving a Saab or a Volvo, commonly seen parked on 60th Street?"

On the beach I notice a tattoo on Sue's thigh as she takes off her tie-dyed cover-up that is cut like overalls, only in shorts.

"I feel like a beached whale," she sighs. Sue's six months pregnant and looks healthy and strong to me. I keep staring at her because she is such an exact replica of her mother, now fifty-two. They have the same dark brown hair, sparkling eyes, and beautiful smile. I know that Gina has been worried about Sue and Will.

"They have nothing, those kids, not even a telephone much of the time. Their house in Tennessee has a space heater in the bedroom, no furnace. Their landlady is nice. She lowers their rent to compensate for the work they do to fix up the house."

Sue and Will work the Renaissance Festivals that travel around the country. Will also works construction for his father, who pays him sporadically. Sue was tiny before her pregnancy, and Gina is happy to see "some meat on those bones."

I suddenly begin to feel uncomfortable—unusual on a beach I have been frequenting since I was a child. People are staring at me as though I were a different person. Is this because I am sitting on a blanket with Gina, Sue, and Will? I try to ignore the discomfort and focus on Bobby, Gina's son and Sue's fifteen-year-old half brother, who has grabbed his boogie board and jumped into the warm but unappealing ocean. It's dark with seaweed, grass, and other salad-like organisms. As the waves curl, they seem to sweep up darker and darker swells.

"He's oblivious," says Gina with a big smile. He doesn't get to the beach very often, and she's pleased that he can finally move freely in the water. Sue and Will announce that they are going for a walk, and Gina and I remain on the blanket to keep an eye on Bobby. Gina relaxes in her deep purple skirted bathing suit. A rosary decorates her neck. She is so white her skin is almost translucent. "Skim milk," she calls herself. She'd been working inside all summer cleaning rental houses on the island. More and more people keep asking her to clean. She's good and she makes decent money, but the work is grueling.

Some Saturdays, her cleaning crews, of three or four people each, have as many as thirteen "changeovers"—thirteen houses to clean between 11:00 A.M. and 2:00 P.M. to get them ready for the next set of weekly renters. Old renters must be out by 11:00; new renters must wait until 2:00 to come in. In that three-hour window, all of the houses must be "changed over"—no small organizational feat for Gina. On Friday night she does the set-ups: mops, brooms, and cleaning supplies for each crew. In summer, she may equip as many as five or six crews.

"Never put two hot-heads on the same crew. Match one each with the cool chicks. Some people like to do kitchens; others bathrooms." She carries a clipboard, but she works right alongside her crews. Kitchens are her specialty. Sometimes her husband, Vinnie, and her best friend, Roberta, who is also part of her church prayer group, head some of the crews; at other times they work right alongside Gina. Gina's and Vinnie's own house, a large, immaculately kept colonial in a tract development carved out of the pinelands, has meticulous landscaping and a vegetable garden. It's kept by Janie, Vinnie's widowed sister, who has lived with them for the past three years, ever since her husband passed away. She has her own room on the second floor. Vinnie is very proud of his plantings and takes real joy in flowers.

Most members of her crews have other jobs as well, but they will drop everything on a busy Saturday to help Gina. Nancy is a real estate agent, and she makes sure to identify herself as such, but everyone knows that real estate is an uncertain business. Aaron, Gina's oldest son, comes down from his job as a trucker up north to help his mom on Saturdays.

Bill, a dark-haired, reserved fellow, works the night shift stocking shelves at the Village Pantry supermarket. His shyness is palpable, and it masks his frustration with his bad luck. He used to have a job at one of the casinos in Atlantic City, but the politics of the casino personnel office left him with a theft charge that is completely unfounded. Bill is completely honest, too honest, in fact, for casino work. The combination of his wife's breast cancer and his own low pay caused them to declare bankruptcy and lose their home. They now rent a small, nine-hundred-square-foot house on the mainland.

Paul, Roberta's husband, supervises maintenance at a retirement home. He's a large, jovial man, whose warmth and kindness permeate all situations. He enjoys solving problems and helping people. His sense of humor enables him to cope with a whole range of difficult situations, from combative Alzheimer's patients to unreasonably demanding nurses. Work and family obligations leave him little time for the beach. He exudes trust, learned and nurtured by his strong family ties and his long years of experience in the construction trades, where people must rely on one another. Paul's twin brother and his family live in the same community. Perhaps being a twin requires tolerance for others.

Other members of the crews are retired and work a few times a week to supplement their incomes. Trent grew up in a coal mining town in Western Pennsylvania. In his twenties he moved to New York, where he worked as a postman for forty years. He likes to talk about his experiences with dogs biting him en route. The retirees rarely work on Saturdays; the pace is too stiff. Gina takes great care to keep the elders safe. Older women don't do stairs.

In winter, work is scarce. Gina works in a law office for a fraction of what she makes cleaning. She has the job because the wife of a member of her cleaning crew has a brother who is an attorney. She uses her networks and they use her. Gina likes having a paycheck each week, but the office job has its frustrations.

"Toilets don't talk back," she stated firmly but jokingly one day.

"What do you mean?"

"I mean just that, Toilets don't talk back," she repeated. "They only make noise when I flush them."

I finally got it. She not only missed the money her cleaning jobs produced; she felt stressed by the office system of authority, by the demands of others. She was not in control there.

I begin to notice that people on the beach are staring at us. Many of them are people I have seen on this beach for forty years. They're summer residents and homeowners who purchased property on the island in the '50s when things were very cheap. "Just a bunch of sand dunes," people used to say. "Nothing there—barely a road on the northern end." The elderly and more affluent summer people now spend winters in Florida, on other islands (called Keys) and along tributaries, where they have equivalent or more elaborate homes. I yearn to go in the water, but it just looks awfully dirty—not inviting in the least. Another day, I tell myself. Just as I have resigned myself to a "no swim" day, Will and Sue return to tell us that the ocean is clean just to the south of the jetty. Would I have thought to look in that direction?

I jump up. "Let's go!" We are on our feet at once, including Jonny, one of my oldest friends and a long-time island summer resident. He's a retired TV producer, a slight, unassuming man with a huge heart. Bobby has gotten out of the water and is walking south with the rest of us.

Bobby, Will, Jonny, and I dive right in. The water is lovely, clear, and warm. Will is much more relaxed. He's smiling as he takes turns sharing the boogie board with Bobby.

"He's digging it!" crows Sue. This is the first time he has ever been in the ocean. Gina hesitates at first, claiming she doesn't want to get her ears wet, but as Jonny gets out, she hands him her rosary to hold along with glasses, towels, etc. Jonny and I take turns holding the things and lifeguarding as Gina and Sue enjoy the water too. As an experienced ocean swimmer I can see the group drifting a little too close to the jetty's large rocks. It's hard to remember how strong the currents are. I wave and shout to them to move over. They obey, but I keep close watch on them. The rocks are covered with sharp barnacles and slippery algae.

As I am standing there, an elderly friend of my mother's calls my name once, then twice. She's taking her daily constitutional and has that determined, and somewhat pinched, look on her face. I see her coming up the beach but am startled by the stern tone of her voice. She talks to me as though she were addressing a child who had just misbehaved badly.

"Is your mother at the beach?"

I decide not to reply, since I feel I am being reprimanded for being with the wrong kind of people. As we walk back to our beach blankets, Sue asks to borrow the beach badges for the weekend. As I hand them to her, I think about the even tighter parking on Saturdays and Sundays. Since my mother's house is close by, I tell Sue where it is.

"Make sure you tell your mother I am coming," admonishes Sue in a very worried tone that causes me to recall my mother's friend's words. I realize that the older woman friend of my mother's was issuing to me a challenge: "What are you doing with those pineys?"

Sue never went back to the beach on the weekend.

A few months later, Sue and Will became the parents of a healthy baby girl, Gina's first grandchild. Gina collected boxes and boxes of "baby stuff" to send with Aaron, her son and Sue's biological brother. Aaron drove his old van halfway across the country to help his sister and her new family fix up their place for the winter. A month after Aaron arrived, Gina and Bobby took a Greyhound bus to Tennessee to see the newest addition to their extended family. Gina reported the ride to be "excruciatingly long but worth it." Aaron has been there for almost a year working in construction with Will.

Gina yearns for the time when Sue can return home with her baby. But it is a long way from Tennessee to the East Coast, and the time and transportation costs are very dear.

A Partridge in a Pear Tree

Crooked River Inn is an old restaurant on the mainland of New Jersey across the bay from the island where Solomon had spent many summers. Now the inn is in a state of rather genteel decline. Brown knotty pine walls look dated and give the place a dark, almost musty, but nonetheless warm feeling. At its height in the 1950s, though, summer boaters would pull up to the dock and settle in for sumptuous lunches: seafood specials, prime rib, clams and oysters on the half shell, right out of the bay. Solomon used to love going there in his fourteen-foot wooden motorboat with the very low freeboard. It was probably the smallest craft to ever carry anyone there. When the bay was choppy, the six-mile crossing was quite treacherous; it was even worse in fog.

He had worked hard for that little boat. Every spring he sanded and sanded the many thin coats of varnish from the deck. It took forever to remove that varnish. Then he painted the varnish back on, coat by thin coat. So great was his enthusiasm for any boat ride that it infected his children, who seized every possible chance for an adventure. They took turns driving the boat. He loved being on the water. He also loved the inn's good food and fine service. The waitresses treated the regulars especially well. As someone who had worked his way through college playing jazz piano in a band in the island's many noisy bars, he felt privilege and joy in these outings.

On this cold December day, almost forty years after the small motorboat had been passed on to another family, Solomon's daughter, Lauren, a professor of pediatrics at a distinguished East Coast medical school, found herself, once again, at the Crooked River Inn. This time, she rode in her friend Gina's car. She and Gina had known each other since their childhood summers on the island, although their lives had taken very different trajectories. Gina had lived on the mainland for many years. She had invited Lauren to this Christmas fund-raiser for the Veterans of Foreign Wars (VFW). Only Gina could get Lauren to attend such an event. Lauren was not at all fond of large gatherings, and her negative memories of veterans' organizations from childhood gave Lauren herself a sense of wonder that she was actually there. The American Legion had a post in her hometown, and she remembered when they gave out awards to worthy high school students. Early on, Solomon, who certainly was not without his prejudices, had taught Lauren that these were, as he put it, a bunch of "flag waving, my country right or wrong people." By this he meant that they operated on a kind of unthinking, blind patriotism that made very difficult the kinds of positive changes Solomon always talked about being needed in America. He had been a lifelong advocate of reforms that benefited the "ordinary man." The gathering at the Crooked River Inn was indeed a collection of "ordinary men (and women)"; politics seemed, somehow, to be suspended on this holiday. It was the first time Lauren had been there without Solomon.

Silver and red balloons clustered on the still knotty pine ceiling in honor of the holiday season. The silver ones tempered the garishness of the traditional red and green decorations. Keyboard music blared over a set of speakers that sounded like they came directly out of a high school auditorium. Karaoke, they now call it. It hurt Lauren's ears; she had always been sensitive to sound. Even her mother's radio programs bothered her in childhood. Today she ignored the noise to concentrate on nostalgia. The same waitresses were still working there, or perhaps their younger sisters, daughters, or nieces. On this particular day, though, they were walking around the large dining room with trays of appetizers—fried zucchini, stuffed mushrooms, "pigs in blankets"—urging the guests to try some. "These are *really* good, honey," they'd coax.

As guests made their way through the entrance, the hostess handed them chips for dinner selections—white for chicken, blue for fish, or red for meat. Very organized and upbeat. In some ways it reminded Lauren of other fund-raisers she had attended. The atmosphere of reserve and formality, ceremoniousness, seemed pervasive, but without the one-upmanship that is so offensive in more upscale events. Everyone smiled, more because of the opportunity to be out in an atmosphere of fellowship and conviviality than for any other reason. The men wore suits, but the women were dressed rather casually—pants, turtlenecks, sweaters. It was not a fashion show, and people were not craning their necks to see who was coming in the door. Gina's friends were there to get out and have a good time, to see one another, and to relax away from the pressures of work, home, and family. Life is hard in the mainland towns in winter; work is scarce outside of the summer resort season, and everyday problems seem to intensify with the dreariness and cold.

In keeping with the spirit of the season, the women were wearing bright red sweaters, the tone of red that makes you think of fresh cherry pie in summer. Paula, Gina's neighbor and occasional member of the cleaning crew, had on a beautiful red cardigan with silver sequins and matching buttons. "Harvé Bernard on sale ten years ago," she confessed proudly. The original price was two hundred dollars, but she picked it up for a little over twenty. It looked stylish with her new haircut and sleek black pants. She has an eye for fashion but doesn't have a chance to use it much; Buck's invalidism ties her down and she hardly ever goes out. He's the father of her daughter; she describes herself as his caregiver, not his wife. Buck has the end stages of multiple sclerosis and taking care of him is itself a full-time job for Paula, who must move him from wheelchair to bed, carry him up- and downstairs, and attend to his every bodily need, including changing diapers, bathing, and feeding. Get him up; lay him down. Her life sounded like a seesaw. She schedules her work around his needs by restricting herself to low-paying part-time and flexible jobs: housekeeper on the island, daycare provider and receptionist in a physician's office near her brother's apartment and her mother's house "up North," in the urban, industrialized part of the state. She has a cup of coffee with her mother after work, washes the kitchen floor, and then goes to pick up her brother's shirts for ironing before driving sixty-five miles south back to her mainland home across from the island. Many nights she doesn't get to bed before 1:00 A.M.

Roberta's red outfit seemed to match her rosy and now blushing cheeks. She cleans only in summer. She likes most to spend time with her grown children and grandbabies. This winter, she was in particular need of cheer because her oldest daughter, son-in-law, and two grandchildren had moved to the Midwest, where her son-in-law had taken a new job. Listening to her, you might have thought they'd moved to Siberia. Gina, who was later to lead the singing, described Roberta as someone she could work with in the same square inch without either of them getting in the other's way. Gina and Roberta have worked together for years in Gina's cleaning business. They are best friends, prayer-group companions, and members of the same mainland community. Gina had on a bright green overblouse that stood out and complemented the sea of red sweaters. She's a slight woman, whose girlish demeanor masks her fifty-four years.

Vinnie, Gina's husband, greeted us with his usual warmth and wouldn't let anyone in our little group pay for dinner. He had organized the festivities and was bustling around making sure everyone was comfortable. Vinnie is Gina's second husband—almost twenty years her senior and father of their fifteen-year-old son. He wants desperately to sell their mainland house and retire to the Pocono Mountains of Pennsylvania where they own a beautiful wooded lot. The taxes in Breckenridge are escalating geometrically, or so it seems to him, and he has spent over a year painting and fixing their house to make it ready for sale. He's a retired gravestone engraver who does a few odd jobs on the side, including helping Gina clean when he is needed on her cleaning crew. Gina is much less enthusiastic about moving and has been praying against the move for several months now; so have many of her crew.

Her cleaning crew is much more than a work group. It's really a small mutual aid society modeled on Gina's childhood. Her mother took in orphans for Catholic Social Services. She sometimes had twenty or more kids in tow. Gina herself goes to Mass every morning, and many of her crew members are members of the church parish. Gina is the spirit behind her cleaning crew. She has a glow. She can motivate people to work when they are dead tired and have fun doing it. She's amazing; organizing and managing the crew is only one of her many talents.

Other members of the crew were there at the inn to celebrate the holiday. Trent, a widower and retired postman, looked dapper in his pressed beige suit and tie. He wanted to sing Polish songs—any songs, not necessarily Christmas carols—but Gina wouldn't let him. He promised Paula, who is also Polish, that he would sing them for her at some other time. His forty-year-old daughter Doris, who, people say, is mildly retarded, accompanied him in her usual awkward way. His strong Polish identity and lively sense of humor get him through a great deal. He's very devoted to his daughter, and he talks about staying away from women so that his daughter will not have to deal with a (wicked) stepmother. Eliza, a member of the parish and occasional crew member, looked at peace in her white, slightly baggy sweater. Lauren was pleased when she came over to give her a hug. She knew Eliza's history of anorexia and her strong sense of obligation to her aged father. Eliza loves jokes—to tell them and to hear them. They are almost stories—long and very complicated, mirrors of her life in the pine barrens. She has a way of talking that makes you sit on the edge of your seat. When she finally comes out with the punch line, listeners feel not only closure, but relief. Eliza smiles broadly—pleased with the joke's impact. For it is her saga retold—her isolated life turned positive and happy. But the veneer of happiness is thin. Gina and Vinnie paid for the dinners of at least six people, maybe more.

The large square banquet tables were set with flowers and bottles of wine. At each place were party favors: a ball-point pen wrapped in clear plastic and a small calculator with the same wrapping.

These seemed to Lauren to be rather serious items, contrasting markedly with the festive, almost frivolous mood of the day. Everyone can use a pen and a calculator.

Across the large table sat Monica, a small, white-haired woman. Lauren had noticed her right away, in part because of her impeccably pressed and delicate cotton lace blouse, but also because of some barely tangible, almost ethereal wisdom and kindliness in her expression. She is almost small enough to be a child, yet she radiates experience, knowledge, and calm. Jon, her "man-friend," sat next to her, and they seemed to belong together. She explained, in some detail, that they both lived in the same trailer park on the mainland, but it was clear that their relationship consisted of more than mere neighborliness and matching heads of white hair. Jon turned out to be the Karaoke king. He could pick out any tune on the piano and attach the appropriate chords. He even had the look of a Santa, without the beard—red cheeks, sparkling blue eyes, and thick, very white hair. Lauren wondered what his story was, especially how he came to love Monica.

A big, intimidating-looking bald man named Paul sat on the other side of the table with a quiet woman who smiled a lot and let him do all the talking. There was something about his affect that was troubling—uncomfortable. He seemed nervous, to be looking over his shoulder, calculating his words. He talked obsessively and loudly. In the sixties, he had owned a sporting goods business on the southern end of the island, a very successful one, or so he claimed. He wanted to impress people, but in a needy sort of way. Floods and storms haunted his memories; he'd had money anxieties after water-soaked merchandise had had to be discarded without any insurance to help make up the loss. He had lost more than one business to the sea. He remembered the old wooden bridge that used to connect the island with the mainland that would flood and take out the brakes of cars. He had crossed it many times. After a few drinks, he talked about disowning his son who had orchestrated drunken parties that left his house in need of costly repairs. Paula was such a sympathetic listener. His whole life story revealed itself before her; he reminded her of Buck in some ways—a dreamer with limited resources, a pretender with a chip on his shoulder. He was the only person at the table who caused Lauren to feel uneasy. He seemed to know, somehow, that Lauren really didn't belong there—didn't fit. Maybe he didn't fit either. Perhaps his experiences on the island had taught him to recognize difference when he came upon it.

As usual, Lauren was trying to keep a low profile. She didn't want to reveal that she lived on the island, at least not to strangers. But her anonymity was short-lived, since Monica turned out to be the mother of a businesswoman she knew well. Monica's daughter, Nan, also a very pleasing person, had often described what it was like growing up in her Polish-Catholic neighborhood in Philadelphia—the long walks to school, the long hours in church, the many delicious foods made by her mother and grandmother on holidays. Their whole extended family was now living on the mainland in small towns, with the exception of one of Nan's nephews, who until recently had rented a house year-round on the island. It was a rather tumble-down place, but he could work in its garage until the neighbors complained. When the landlord sold the property and the new owner removed the old house, he moved into an apartment on the fishing dock next to the deli. There he used a small space to work in his boat repair business. He knows boats and motors, almost intuitively, as though he were born to be on the water. His reputation is strong up and down the coast. Unlike the rest of his family, he was determined to stay on the island close to the sea and the bar that serves fishermen and tourists alike. It's a rather unique place; it's old and homey, with roaring fires in the big fireplaces in winter. Everyone feels comfortable within its dark wooden walls. The waitresses call everyone "honey," and they remember what you drink. It's owned by two couples, both from old island families in one real estate business. They serve great burgers, fish, clams, and chowders.

Monica's family had left Philadelphia in the early sixties and moved to rural South Jersey. Monica's youngest daughter is a nurse who monitors her mother's health closely. Monica talks about each daughter contributing a little something to her life. She is a very vigorous woman who still spends some time working as a housekeeper on the island. It turned out that Monica also knew Lauren's elderly and now quite frail great-aunt, Eloise. In fact, Monica had traveled with Eloise to Arizona in the 1980s after Eloise's husband had passed away. She knew the family history, including the fact that the wealthy couple had purchased several large tracts of land on the northern end of the island in the 1940s. People thought they were crazy to invest in such a place. But the land was very cheap, and Eloise always had a head for business. In those days, to venture so far away from established towns was simply not done. Monica's son-in-law, Roy, had been building houses for Eloise's family for almost thirty years. He was the best builder on the island. He even built a bayfront house for his own family in one of the more exclusive northerly island communities. It was an extraordinary house— very large and fortress-like, with a special wood-and-stained-glass door at the entrance to the master bedroom. A curved, raised counter in the kitchen made of gorgeous red oak could have been featured in a magazine like *Architectural Digest* or *Fine Homebuilding*. It was a real masterpiece. He had put his craftsman's soul into that house, but he never felt at home there. One neighbor asked him whether he would grade his driveway; another wanted Roy to landscape his yard. They made him feel like a common laborer, not a fellow homeowner. He sold his creation five years after he built it and moved to the mainland.

As the banquet wore on and the coffee was being served, Monica moved around the table to talk more privately with Lauren, who confessed, with as much tact and diplomacy as she could muster, that she and Aunt Eloise had never had very good communication. Monica replied with a smile, "Does she communicate well with anyone?" It was such a quick reply that Lauren was surprised by the cutting humor. It created instant empathy between them. Monica proceeded to tell stories of nearly twenty years ago, stories one does not ordinarily hear at banquets. On her first trip to Phoenix with Eloise, Monica had accompanied her to a fancy restaurant for lunch. It was never clear to Monica whether Eloise regarded her as a friend, a servant, or some combination of the two. Nonetheless, without consultation, Eloise had insisted on sharing a very small sandwich. Monica finished lunch hungry and humiliated. After three days, Monica escaped home.

Lauren herself had always felt uneasy in Eloise's presence. Everything she did was scrutinized closely and criticized. If she did one thing, it was wrong. If she did the opposite, she was also blamed. In their section of Phoenix, every other car seemed to be a Rolls Royce or a Mercedes. It may be one of the few towns in the country to boast of *public* clay tennis courts. But it was not the affluent setting that had bothered Monica, it was Eloise's tense and patronizing manner that combined with her power to manipulate people by putting them in a "damned if you do and damned if you don't" position. Eloise never gave a straight answer or a clear and honest reason. Even when you offered to do something kind for her she would twist it into something negative. She was also very demanding and rigid in a passive-aggressive way, trumping up illnesses, for example, or creating a crisis just to get attention. Lauren remembered the time she demanded that a grandchild with a new driver's license drive her to the doctor in the city from the island. When Lauren volunteered to do it, Eloise was suddenly well. These experiences with Eloise's need for power and control had taught Lauren to keep her distance. Monica's reaction to her had been simply to flee.

As the intensity of their conversation grew, Lauren could sense Paul trying to listen in; Monica was careful to keep her voice down. The details of her experience in Arizona seemed right at the front of her memory, as though the events had happened recently, not twenty years in the past. She seemed to need to talk with someone about it, and Lauren was a sympathetic listener. Paula and Roberta were sharing stories too, and there was a large audio speaker right next to their table muffling conversation and causing some people to shout over the music. Still, Lauren could feel people staring at her. Was it that she was a stranger? Was it her intent expression and her watchfulness in this unfamiliar setting? Was it that she was so clearly an out-sider, regardless of the fact that she knew many of the people in the room?

Jon continued playing the keyboard with heart. He was warm-ing up for the caroling that was about to begin. Gina took the mike and began leading the singing. A mixture of solos by Gina and Jon and their encouragement of group participation com-bined to create a light-hearted feeling. Lauren had to turn her chair so that she was not sitting with her back to the musicians. Gina was working hard but enjoying every minute. She had placed photocopies of the words to the carols on each table. She knew how to please the crowd and how to get people to join in.

"The Twelve Days of Christmas" was last. Each table was assigned a different day. Gina set up a competition. The table with the loudest and most enthusiastic voices would win a prize. Lauren's and Monica's table was first, which meant that their part, "a partridge in a pear tree," the gift on the first day of Christmas, was repeated more than any other phrase in the song.

Since Gina had been sitting at this first table, her enthusias-tic gaze seemed to radiate right to it. As the verses proceeded, the voices became stronger and stronger. At one point, about midway through the song, someone at the table motioned for all at the table to stand up when it was time for "a partridge in a pear tree." The enthusiasm paid off. The prize went to Monica, the oldest person at the table. It was a tray painted in red and green.

EPILOGUE

Lauren felt relieved that she had survived the banquet without too much awkwardness. At the very least, she had expected standoffishness. But there was great tolerance of difference and warmth among the banquet goers, perhaps because they had already been through so much.

While it would not be true to say that Lauren was relaxed, she was very grateful for the chance to talk with Monica at such length. It was a kind of catching up along class lines that rarely happens except by chance. Gina had provided the context, and to see Gina perform with such talent and grace gave Lauren pleasure, almost the pleasure of a close relative watching a sister transcend the mundane, daily drudgery of housecleaning for just a few short hours. She understood why Gina went to Mass every morning. Lauren also began to think that Gina now occupied the place where Solomon's father had been situated early in his life. If going to the inn took Lauren back to her own childhood, watching Gina felt like a kind of class memory. She began to think of the connections between her family and Gina's. Lauren's grandfather loved the violin but had to spread wallpaper for a living.

27

A Partridge
in a
Pear Tree

A wonderful lobster dinner. Just Chris, short for Christiana, Noah, and Lauren, Noah's mom. Chris and Noah had been together for their entire last year of high school. This was the summer before their freshman year of college. Lauren felt honored to be included. Chris had arrived that very day, and she and Noah had not seen each other for almost six weeks. Linn, a close family friend, had picked her up in Philadelphia, a two-hour drive from the island. Whenever the family needed a helping hand, Linn was there. Chris came laden with delicious ice cream packed in dry ice from a famous candy shop and ice cream parlor in their home town. Among the several flavors, only the orange sorbet had liquefied, but the rest remained semi-frozen: raspberry and mocha chip, with huge chunks of dark chocolate candy embedded in the rich ice cream.

Noah had wanted a special small, quiet dinner, not the usual collection of friends and relatives that congregated for dinner on the large screened porch overlooking the bay between the island and the mainland. He had always been a sensitive child, a person who chose his words carefully and who knew what would make occasions special. The three of them had just finished sharing two huge lobsters that had required not just lobster crackers, but a hammer and cutting board as well. They had wrapped the huge claws in dish towels before placing them on the wooden cutting board for the hammer strike.

Lobster was Chris's favorite food. She had spent the first nine years of her life living in Martha's Vineyard, and she loved everything about the seashore, including ocean lifeguards like Noah, whose dark curly hair and bronzed skin were set off by deep-set light eyes. Noah was also very fond of lobster, and it was difficult to tell which he was enjoying more, the lobster or Chris's beautiful smile and upbeat presence. They laughed and joked as they struggled to eat the messy food with some semblance of decorum.

The cleanup was lengthy as two large smelly pots had to be washed along with dishes and implements. The three of them accomplished the tasks quickly, with an ease that comes with familiarity. They were relieved to be finished with the strenuous eating. Lauren was delighted to have such a lovely young woman in their dominantly male house. She had known Chris for over a year and welcomed her as a member of the family.

They were just about to break out the ice cream when the phone call interrupted: medical emergency at 23 Berry Drive, home of Lauren's elderly parents—Noah's grandparents.

Lauren knew instantly that the night was not going to end well. They rushed into Noah's car for the half-mile trip north— a short drive that they had done thousands of times. Emergency vehicles and police cars stood in front of the house with their lights still flashing. Sophia, ashen, was sitting on the edge of Solomon's brown leather chair. Her white cotton peasant dress that often doubled as a nightgown made her look even whiter as she watched the paramedics bend over Solomon's body on the kitchen floor. His stomach was swollen and his face was distorted. The normally benign tremor in Sophia's hands was uncontrollable; she was too stunned to cry.

"I called 911. Chip was the first one here. He kept telling Solomon to hold on. He's a saint. He's so calm and caring. He came right away."

Chip's a police officer who lives across the street from Solomon and Sophia. Lauren remembers him as a teenager doing odd jobs in the neighborhood. "Chippy," everyone called him. The diminutive had always had a certain patronizing twinge to it. It certainly didn't apply now to this large, strong man, whose inner strength was even more impressive than his large, muscular frame. Chip's family had lived on the street for over fifty years, summer and winter. His father was a builder and his mother a nurse. His two sisters, Sally and Judy, used to baby-sit for Lauren's two boys. Sally and Judy are not twins; Sally is much taller and more talkative, with an angular, not a round face, but some people on the street couldn't tell them apart. Lauren often wondered why this was so. Why did some people refuse to regard them as separate individuals?

People on Berry Street always talked about the family warmly but with a certain sense of distance in their voices. To live on the island year-round was regarded by summer people with disdain. The city (New York or Philadelphia) was considered the font of culture and opportunity as well as the location of good schools, hospitals, museums, and symphony orchestras. The island, especially in the '50s and '60s, was too isolated from the culture of the city.

Chip and the paramedics worked for longer than necessary. They used the paddles and bagged Solomon. Periodically, they called the station to give an update on his condition. They could not get a heartbeat. His stomach was even more distended and his color was gray. Lauren knew he was not coming back. Noah looked on with great concentration. He said nothing. He's a lifeguard trained in CPR, so he was familiar with many of the procedures. He's also very strong. If Solomon had been on that screened porch for dinner, as he normally was, Noah would have been the one to try to resuscitate him; he would have failed. All of these thoughts were going through Lauren's mind as she tried to assess the situation and decide what should be done next.

Sophia had been in their bedroom when she heard a crashing sound in the kitchen. Apparently, Solomon had hit his head after collapsing in front of the open refrigerator. There were condiment bottles everywhere and the shelf on the refrigerator door was hanging as if by a thread.

When the paramedics left, Chip stayed. So did his fellow police officer and buddy, Stan. They put the ketchup and mustard back in the refrigerator. They covered Solomon with a sheet, as Lauren could not bear to see him lying there. She had been to too many funerals with open caskets. Chip called the funeral home to come and retrieve the body and offered to wait in the house. Chip and Stan took care of things beyond their official obligations.

Lauren made the first essential phone calls—first to her husband, who was out of town, then to her brother in Denver, then to Sophia's brother in San Francisco. Their family was small, tiny, in fact. It was also very spread out. Solomon had only one younger brother, who had passed away fifteen years earlier. He had not seen his half brother in twenty-five years.

Lauren left with Sophia, Noah, and Chris, who had been waiting in the car all of this time. She had been introduced to Sophia and Solomon just that afternoon. They went back to the house with the screened porch. Lauren put Sophia in her bed. She wanted to keep her close, afraid, perhaps, that she would become hysterical. She didn't that night, but she didn't sleep either. The next day, as friends began to call and come to Lauren's house to offer condolences, a physician friend wrote out a prescription for Valium. Lauren kept the pills on hand, just in case. But Sophia was strong.

More and more phone calls. Sophia dictated the list of people who needed to be called. She was incapable of talking to her brother or her best friend from childhood. The closer the person, the more difficult it was to talk. Lauren made some calls and fielded others. Joshua, Lauren's older son, had been very close to Solomon. From the time he was a small child, he followed Solomon around and became involved in Solomon's many projects: electronics, boats, household repair. When Solomon died, Josh was in Alaska working on a fishing boat. In order to reach him, an operator at a cannery on shore would have to radio the captain of the boat. Lauren and her husband decided that it was best to wait until Josh came ashore and called home. Why provide bad news with no one on the other end of the line? But Josh's absence became very palpable in this time of crisis. He and Solomon had become soul mates, and they probably always will be in some spiritual way. They both loved music, especially jazz. They both had a special inventive kind of creativity. They thought a lot about new devices. For Solomon it had been radios and record players in the '40s and '50s, when he started a small electronics company. For Josh it is computers, music, and virtual reality—all three really, in new combinations and applications. Solomon had missed Josh a great deal. His life had been enriched enormously by his young grandson—everything from attending his crew regattas to sharing musical stories about jazz greats. It was the first summer that Josh had been away from the island and from the family. During Josh's absence, Solomon had gone to great lengths to research the Alaskan fishing scene. He learned the schedule of the boats, where the canneries were located, and the nature of the relationships between boats and canneries. Solomon was persistent that way. He had his ways of being with Josh, albeit from a distance. Somehow the combination of Solomon's demise and Josh's absence created a noticeable vacuum in this already small family.

The evening after Solomon died, Lauren received a phone call from Chris's mother, a person she had met briefly at various school functions. As a busy professional, Lauren had little time for socializing with the mothers of her children's friends. She didn't belong to the garden club or the country club, or the Parent-Teachers Association, for that matter. They had never had a real conversation.

"I have arranged a plane ticket for Chris, since I don't want her to impose herself on your family."

"Impose herself?" Lauren queried. "She is a blessing. Please don't feel that she must leave, unless, of course, she feels she wants to. She is such a help and a real comfort for Noah."

They talked for some time. Lauren put down the phone thinking, "What a lovely conversation. No wonder Chris is such a caring person."

Neighbors and friends began to appear even before Lauren's brother, Alan, could get to the island from Denver where he and his wife, Marlene, had busy law practices. Sophia received visitors on the screened porch, her way of mourning in private, in a safe and beautiful setting. Lauren always had a pot of healthy soup on the stove and a salad in the refrigerator. People came with cakes, a traditional way of showing condolences. By the time Alan and Marlene arrived, they were a day behind in the mourning process, and it took several days before they were able to catch up. Perhaps the fact that they were not there to witness the attempts to resuscitate Solomon made it more difficult for them to accept the death? Perhaps their anxiety had accumulated and built during the long trip east? Perhaps Alan's level of sentimentality was higher than Lauren's and Sophia's?

One of Sophia's more conventional friends came into Lauren's kitchen to tell her that she had informed the rabbi of Solomon's death. The small Jewish community center on the southern end of the island was just that, small. The rabbi wanted to announce Solomon's death at Friday night services. He called Lauren's house, wanting to confirm the details. Lauren had to be the person to inform him that Sophia did not want any public recognition. She was not ready to inform the community, and she wanted to grieve in private. The rabbi did not seem to understand. He tried to talk Lauren into the announcement. The more he tried, the more she resisted, and the higher the level of tension in their conversation. How crass to attempt a hard sell at a time like this!

Lauren knew that Solomon would have said that the rabbi was just trying to keep his job. Solomon had always had a cynical view of religion that was accompanied by his sharp, analytical wit. After all, the rabbi served a privileged group of rather traditional and conservative people, in both the religious and the political senses. Solomon's irreverence was something Lauren remembered as a child. His grace before dinner: "Good bread, good meat, good God, let's eat." His philosophy during the High Holy Days: "I don't believe in religion of the stomach." He never fasted on Yom Kippur. His commentaries comparing rabbis to car salesmen and his notions that rabbis were self-promoting and self-centered came into Lauren's mind as she tried, with great difficulty, to muster diplomacy and tact.

Jell-O with artificial whipped cream entered Lauren's kitchen of natural whole foods. It appeared in a very fancy pan, complete with a matching cover. This offering came from a wealthy island woman who was the wife of a corporate executive. Cloth napkins accompanied the dish—as decoration, Lauren supposed. Knowing how chagrined Lauren was, Jonny, an old friend, volunteered that he liked Jell-O and would polish it off in a day or two. She stored it on the very bottom shelf of the refrigerator in a place where she had to bend to see it. Cakes and cookies were brought by island people. A very thin woman brought a so-called "health cake" that tasted like cardboard. Another brought a coffee cake that was so ordinary, it might have come from a supermarket bakery. There were so many cakes, in fact, that Lauren began redistributing them by sending large pieces home with people. Another friend of Sophia's brought fancy crackers and a mustard dip. Others brought pasta and condiments packed in a basket that was half-filled with straw. Only Nan, Lauren's friend from the mainland, brought "real food": delicious vegetable salads, chicken salad, and whole-grain bread. Alan, Lauren, and Maureen stayed up late one night chopping vegetables for another caldron of soup. The cooking provided therapy for all of them, and a good chance to talk. Lauren's friends, Jonny and his wife, Jane, who had recently been diagnosed with a terminal disease, stayed by Lauren's side. They came to the house every day; they did dishes and helped serve. Keeping busy with the daily chores of living distracted everyone from Solomon's sudden death and from the inevitability of Jane's.

Many people came and stayed for hours and, of course, they were fed. They expected meals to be served. Some came with relatives in tow who were served with generosity and grace. Some stayed for lunch and dinner. There were also special diets to accommodate. Tom, a childhood friend of Sophia's, with his heart condition, could not have salt. Mushroom barley soup for him. He was a talker too, dominating the conversation with stories of his own family's history. These stories always had the same subtext: his family was better than any other. So in addition to feeding him and caring for his special needs, Lauren had to put up with his relentless egotism.

At the time Lauren was too busy keeping Sophia occupied to think about these issues; she welcomed company for her grieving mother. But in retrospect, she felt invaded and even exploited by the so-called community. How dare Tom insert himself into this delicate situation? How dare he assume that his views were shared by all around the table. Many of Lauren's friends had married outside of their faiths and ethnicities, but Tom seemed oblivious to these facts even when these friends were sitting across the table. His stories, while interesting in some respects, seemed inappropriate in their crassness and naïveté. No one was asking about his life history—his trials, his triumphs over the odds—yet he felt impelled to tell it.

In another context, and at another time, Lauren might have relished the detail, but the detail was tainted with prejudice. "Hard work conquers all," he repeated, over and over. Not at her dinner table. Solomon would have steered the conversation in another direction. He was one of those people who not only could cross class and ethnic boundaries with ease but also had a deeply felt appreciation of difference. So-called outsiders were just as important to him as so-called insiders who were following ritual, but bringing little, actually or symbolically. Solomon hated meaningless ritual. He would have used humor, sarcasm, whatever seemed most effective to counter prejudice of any sort. Solomon would not have allowed class prejudice to be expressed in his house.

EPILOGUE

Sophia's first wedding anniversary without Solomon. She proudly took her regular walk at the lighthouse pier even though it was raining quite heavily. She reported to Lauren that her friend Marian called to cancel the walk but that she went anyway. Later in the day she talked about the importance of attitude, of "counting your blessings." Lauren was quite aware that this day would be difficult, so she made sure to keep a close eye on Sophia.

Lauren was pleased when Sophia called to see whether her daughter had done her errands yet. While Sophia was clearly capable of picking up her own dry cleaning, she wanted an outing with company. When they stopped to pick up some clothing that Sophia had ordered at a local boutique, Sophia announced that she had just bought herself an anniversary present. When Lauren looked over to her in the passenger seat of the car she could see that Sophia had started to cry.

"Let's not both start bawling," Lauren said half jokingly but at the same time fighting tears herself.

Sophia had announced earlier that she was going to services with some friends and that she had plenty of food to eat at home, but as Lauren was taking Sophia's packages into her house she pictured Sophia sitting and eating her dinner by herself at her kitchen table on her first anniversary without Solomon.

"No," she thought, this would be a very bad idea. It was almost two hours until Sophia's friends would pick her up for services.

"Call your friends and ask them to pick you up at my house," Lauren gently ordered in a somewhat tentative voice. "I have salad all made at home."

This tactic worked, as Sophia loved to eat salads but hated to make them. She came and ate her fill of salad and vegetarian lasagna, complete with banana bread and fresh peaches for the finish.

Lauren could not help but think: here are close friends offering to take Sophia to services. Why did they not ask her to dinner?

Linn, a large, cheery woman from the mainland town of Morgan-town, drives Lauren from the island to the closest airport—about a two-hour drive, one way. Ordinarily, Lauren would take her own car, but she wants to talk to Linn, and she knows the extra money will come in handy for her. Lauren has arranged a visit to her son on the West Coast to dovetail with a professional meeting. Combining business and pleasure is usually difficult, but this time, Lauren has decided to take some time away from work. It's very hot for an October day, and Linn apologetically describes the van's air conditioning as "permanently broken." Lauren sheds her linen jacket. Rushing to get ready has overheated her enough.

For Linn, chauffeuring is a second, part-time job. She juggles driving with her family responsibilities and with her part-time accounting work at a printing company, the only copy center on the island. She delights in playing with numbers and details and can prepare the payroll in almost no time. The flexible hours can be long, and she knows she has to be very organized and work very hard to get everything done. She's an energetic person, though, with an organizational chart in her head. Her daughter, Judy, who is at the moment a disappointment to Linn, received her schooling at home under Linn's supervision. She now works at Wal-Mart. Judy's plans do not include college, and Linn calls working at Wal-Mart for $6.00 an hour a dead-end job. Judy still lives at home but is, of course, subject to her parents' rules and restrictions. Friends can visit only on a limited basis. Meals are free, but rent must be paid to Dad each month. Linn's son attends the local high school, where, so far, he gets good grades. Linn worries about whether he will finish, though.

Linn can earn quite a bit of money driving the elderly, retired summer people who now spend more and more time on the island. She will cheerfully drive friends, relatives, and neighbors of her regular customers as well. Her price varies according to her relationship with her passengers. Friends are not charged, although they usually insist on paying for gasoline. People she doesn't know or doesn't like get charged exorbitantly. Lauren's cranky great-aunt Eloise has to pay top dollar, and even then Linn complains constantly about her demanding personality.

The previous week, Linn and her husband, Bill, who works for the telephone company, had driven Lauren's mother, Sophia, from the island to High Holy Day services in the city. After suffering from chronic congestive heart failure following a stroke six years earlier, Sophia's husband and Lauren's father, Solomon, had died suddenly in mid-July. He would have celebrated his eightieth birthday that next January. Bill had been close to Solomon. He had been a friend and colleague more than an employee. When Bill finished his landscaping work in Solomon's yard, he would sit in the living room and visit; they spent hours talking about a range of issues, switching back and forth from one topic to another—everything from the newest telephone technology to Bob's relationships with his co-workers. They had been buddies, of sorts, for nearly fifteen years. Solomon was a retired electronics engineer, and he loved to talk shop. Bill and Linn felt the loss of Solomon. He was not close to many people.

Sophia had been nervous about bringing non-Jews to the large, suburban synagogue, especially on the High Holy Days. It was very crowded—large families with children dressed in beautiful, expensive, uncomfortable clothes. Men and women sat together. It was not orthodox. But Bill and Linn were happy to take her. It was a new cultural experience for them. In fact, they commented to Sophia that they had enjoyed the service, especially the music, immensely. As fundamentalist Christians, Bill and Linn devoted much of their lives to spirituality. They had never been inside a synagogue, though, and the familiarity of the service surprised them.

Lauren, who, if one had to give her a religious-sounding label, might be called a "secular humanist," had great difficulty understanding why Sophia was so adamant about going all the way to the city to synagogue when a perfectly fine little temple sat on the populated southern end of the island. Once on the island, Lauren always did her best to remain there for as long as possible. Although Lauren was, at best, ambivalent about going to synagogue at all, she would have accompanied Sophia to the local services. It was intimate; many of Sophia's close friends would be there, and it would avoid the trip to the city. But Sophia insisted on going to the modern, impersonal monument of a synagogue where she had few, if any, close friends. Lauren refused to go.

In September, fewer than two months after Solomon's death, Sophia placed Solomon's name in the large synagogue's Book of Remembrances. She did this after discovering that he had made a substantial donation to the memorial fund there. Sophia claimed proudly that he had gotten more religious over the years. It was true that he went to services with Sophia whenever she wanted to go.

"He really mellowed in his old age," she insisted with great pleasure and just a hint of smugness.

To Lauren this sounded preposterous; Solomon had been an atheist all his life. In his youth he had been a devoted member of the Ethical Culture Society, an important, radical, pre–World War II social movement that included the founding of several progressive schools for working-class children on the East Coast. His was an intellectualized sort of religion that emphasized philosophy and ethics, not ritual and convention. As a young adult, Solomon had lost employment because he was a member of the Communist Party. The House Un-American Activities Committee (HUAC) had investigated him in the fifties for his collection of Al Jolson recordings. Sophia remembers federal officials questioning her neighbors as to their patriotism. Lauren shared and admired his free thinking, especially his disdain for "meaningless ritual," a favorite phrase of his. Religious? No. Lauren remembers Solomon conceding to attend High Holy Day services, but she always thought of it as a gesture of companionship, so that Sophia would not have to go alone.

He had not embraced religion all of a sudden. Rather, it seemed to Lauren that he must have made the donation in order to enhance his prestige in the community. What better evidence of his financial well-being than to afford giving to this upscale synagogue? He had, after all, grown up in the ghetto. His father had been a poor immigrant from the former Soviet Union and his mother had come from Poland. Solomon's move to this affluent community had been a step up.

While Sophia was greatly comforted by Linn and Bill, she was upset because they had refused to take any money for the trip to the synagogue. She and Linn had not been nearly as close as Solomon and Bill. Sophia wanted to maintain a separation between herself and "them." She saw herself as a college-educated person with a professional job complete with benefits and a good pension. Security. She saw Linn and Bill as people of lesser status, with lesser jobs and fewer resources. Insecurity. Sophia had a tendency to want to settle her debts. She never wanted to be "beholden" to anyone.

"We did it as friends," Linn tells Lauren as they drive through the back roads on the way to the airport.

"Your mom was very teary when they talked about the deceased at the service," she adds.

"What happened after the service when you went to the house?" Lauren asks, with some trepidation. The trip to the synagogue was also coupled with Sophia's first return as a widow to their home of forty-five years.

"We talked to her a lot," Linn answers. "She said she had to stay focused on her list of things to do. You know, like finding the title to Solomon's old Mercedes."

Lauren thinks about Sophia's ability to focus—a coping strategy even if it blocked out both emotion and rationality. The Mercedes served as a symbol of Solomon's love for status and comfort. He took great pleasure in driving it and acted as though it were brand new. His gadgets occupied the dashboard—radar detector, CD player, battery charger, and other stuff. The old car sat low to the ground, just like he did. He always kept it in their locked garage.

Linn continues with her report to Lauren. "We got the mail and we found the serial number on the piano. We knew this was the first time Sophia had returned to their house without him."

Solomon had been a talented pianist. Sophia took great pride in this fact, and would mention it whenever she had an opening in a conversation. He had opted, instead of pursuing a career in music, to attend the university as a member of the "X-Group," an honors program in which students could take as many courses as they wanted, with no limits and no requirements. Solomon loved it. He always had a free intellectual spirit.

Lauren is heartened and relieved by Linn's sensitivity and caring. Linn's own mother had died in 1991 of Lou Gehrig's disease. Her sister had died of ovarian cancer just six months earlier, at the age of thirty-one. Her father, who took care of her mother until the end, has his own life now.

"We don't know much about his life, and we're waiting for the day when he tells us. We have other parents, you know, older people like your parents, Solomon and Sophia."

Lauren's relief turns instantly to understanding. So that was it: Sophia and Solomon were surrogate parents. They had been for some fifteen years. Lauren was amazed that Linn and Bill had so much time for them. But Linn proceeds to talk about how she never wanted to work full-time. She had too many other things she wanted to do. Lauren begins exploring these other things with Linn. She wants to change the subject away from her father's death, and she is intrigued by Linn's sense of calm.

"We have a ministry," Linn continues. The mere mention of a ministry piques Lauren's curiosity. Her own community work has given her experience with people who have received help from various ministries as well as with people who create and manage social services. "It's called the 'Teacup Ministry.'"

"Will you tell me about the Teacup Ministry?" Lauren asks

tentatively, thinking to herself what a wonderful name it is.

"Oh, we bring needy people tea in teacups—tea and bread. We make the bread."

"What kind of bread?"

"You know, cinnamon or whole wheat, healthy stuff. We don't want to pass out junk."

"Do you go alone?"

"We go in pairs. We ask people whether they have any prayer wishes. This is how we learn what they need. If people are not too receptive, we leave food on the doorstep."

"How many people are involved in the Teacup Ministry?"

"About eight, but it's growing. We go all over Pacific and Suncoast Counties, but not Framingham County. That's too far."

Lauren's curiosity is growing. This creative, informal social service network seems somehow very traditional but also innovative.

"What about social workers?" she asks, somewhat tentatively.

Linn replies definitively. "There are none. You have to be on welfare. We try to help people so they can get back on an even keel. Most people just go through tough times; then they recover. I know from experience. You know that Billy was fired from his job at the telephone company. He was out of work for two years. He was accused of sabotage. Then, shortly after that, he fell off a roof and was almost killed. It took him months and months to recover."

Lauren acknowledges that she knew he had been out of work, but that she hadn't realized it had been for two years.

"It was very rough. The guys at work put together the Sunshine Fund and they did a raffle to collect money. We paid it all back though, but we shouldn't have. It was a lot of money, over $100 a week. This is why I do the Teacup Ministry. It can happen to anybody. You never know when a helping hand is needed or in what form."

Sophia had been a recipient of the Teacup Ministry.

EPILOGUE

Several months—in fact, almost a year after Solomon's death—Sophia called upon Linn to drive her to several places within the area to do some errands. Sophia will drive locally, but she is uncomfortable driving on interstate highways.

Linn then called upon Sophia to co-sign a loan for her daughter Judy's car, an old Chevy that had belonged to a friend of a friend on the mainland. It seems that in the aftermath of her husband's employment problems, they had given up credit cards and lost their ability to receive credit. Linn's daughter made several trips from her home on the mainland to Sophia's home to shuffle the paperwork. Judy was clearly uncomfortable in Sophia's house. She avoided eye contact and seemed to want to leave as soon as possible. She came in Linn's van, which, she confessed, she hated to drive.

Linn is no longer working at the printing company. She talked about starting her own business, but she never did. She spent several summer months cleaning houses on the island, after which they lost their house to bankruptcy. Perhaps the Teacup Ministry was costing her too much.

The City House

That morning was frigid and damp, as the seashore can be in late November. Lauren, who was reluctantly taking some time off from her busy pediatric practice, already had negative feelings about the long drive from the island to the city for the eye doctor's visit for her recently widowed mother, Sophia. The tedious bleakness of the road and the increasing density of the traffic as they approached the urban fringes combined with a certain tension between mother and daughter. Perhaps it was just the normal tensions between women of different generations. Perhaps it was also that they were dealing with Solomon's death so differently.

As they drove west on the long desolate road, Sophia asked, "Did you see the sunrise? It was beautiful." She meant it, but somehow Lauren always read the subtext—something like: "I was up at dawn, what were you doing asleep?" Sophia had always had a strong work ethic and she prided herself on her energetic routine. Somehow her routine seemed even more rigid than ever, perhaps to fill the day so that feelings would not have any space or time. Yet, as they were driving Sophia was dozing off, snoring even, obviously exhausted by nine o'clock in the morning.

Fortunately traffic was light. They arrived early for the appointment and took seats. The eye doctor, a tall man, now sixty and white haired, gave Lauren a warm smile and handshake.

"How are you? It's been so many years."

"Hi, Mark. Yes it has."

She could feel his patients' ears perk up at her use of his first name. Lauren and Mark had grown up together in the same summer island community, although he was close to a decade older than she. The last time Lauren had seen him, his hair was thick and black; in fact, she remembers him as looking very much like her own two sons do now, tan and muscular, adult, but young. The fluorescent light of the office in November made his pale face and thinning hair contrast even more starkly with her memory. Mark's father, dead now for over twenty years, had been an ophthalmologist in that same tiny office in Monroe, a neighborhood of small houses and narrow streets in Northeast Philadelphia. Sophia explained that Mark's family used to live there, above the office, but they moved to upscale Center City many years ago. Until last year, Rita, Mark's mother, had driven from Center City on the expressway to spend her usual one day a week as Mark's receptionist. Before that, she had worked in the office full-time. She knew the patients by name and she knew their histories. Just before her eightieth birthday, she decided that the drive was too much for her.

Outside, a small and modest black and white sign announced the presence of a doctor's office. The sign was really the only feature that distinguished this row house from all of the others in the neighborhood. There are two doctors now: Mark's partner is a young Asian American doctor who recently completed his residency. A white-haired nurse greeted white-haired patients who indeed waited patiently on the benches and hard wooden chairs that line the walls of the small waiting room. The place was austere, but Lauren could imagine that fifty years ago, when Mark's father was starting his practice, it must have seemed substantial. Row houses do have a certain solidity to them.

The waiting room held several elderly couples. The men walked in shuffles just as Sophia's husband, Solomon, had before he died. Lauren could feel Sophia looking at them, yearning for Solomon. The women were more robust and much livelier than the men. They walked with assurance, assisting the men with car keys and coats. It was difficult to discern which

Eastern European languages were being spoken. Polish was one, but the others were unfamiliar to Lauren. A sense of old worldliness seemed to take the waiting room back to the past, almost as if one were seeing snapshots of the last century. Lauren wondered where the adult children of these elderly people might be. Did they still live in the neighborhood, or were they thousands of miles away? Perhaps they were merely at work during this weekday morning?

"Dr. Lee is in the downtown office," said one of the nurses in to the telephone. The office downtown is plush and serves a different clientele. Mark spends only one day a week in Monroe. Lauren wondered whether it was his community service. How long would he keep seeing patients there?

"Give my regards to your mother, Mark," Sophia said as she exited the examining area.

The visit was over quickly, and Lauren and Sophia proceeded to their errands. As they were driving out of Monroe, toward the suburbs, Lauren kept thinking about how decades of slow transformations must have affected the composition of this neighborhood. Indeed, it had changed greatly since Mark's family had lived there. Immigrants from the same country tend to group themselves in the same neighborhoods, often in a series of blocks. When one group moves out, usually to better circumstances, another group moves in. Then Lauren's thoughts were interrupted by Sophia, who began to list their day's itinerary. It included a visit to their city house, which was in a suburb north of Monroe.

The cable TV box had to be returned in order for the service to be cut off and the charges to be stopped, including the charge for the rental of the cable box itself, a sum of about $150. Sophia insisted that the return of the box required a trip to an office beyond the northern suburbs. Lauren kept thinking that there must be a more efficient way to accomplish the task—by phone or at an office closer to Sophia's home—but at this point, she was only the chauffeur. After Lauren and Sophia stood in line for some time, they were informed that this was not the right office or even the right cable company. The woman behind the window explained the mistake with a certain amount of professionalism, but with an eye toward the long line of people who were shifting from one foot to the other behind Sophia. While Lauren felt somewhat vindicated that the trip had been a waste of time, she also had to deal with Sophia's persistent efforts to settle her affairs and to reach closure on all of the tasks associated with her city house. Lauren was tempted to pay the $150 herself, just so the task would be completed. But Sophia, a child of the Great Depression, was not willing to have anyone part with such a sum of money. She resolved to go home and make some phone calls.

Solomon had been known to buy all sorts of electronic "toys." Put him in Wal-Mart or Radio Shack and he could easily spend hours buying multiple small items, from Walkman radios and headphones to plugs and night lights. He was like a kid in a high-tech candy store. But he was secretive about his stashes of batteries and Walkman radio parts. He never told Sophia about these purchases. It wasn't just the cable box, though. Enormous credit card bills would arrive to surprise Sophia—no single item was very expensive, but many small items added up. Recalling her anger at his careless spending was making her agitated.

She was having conflicting feelings though, for he had been a very giving man, and she preferred, in her mind's fresh memory, to emphasize his generosity. Sophia was, in fact, wearing a pair of $400 earrings she had bought for herself a few months after he died.

"He would have wanted me to have these," Sophia announced with tears in her eyes as she and Lauren were standing in a very expensive gallery in suburban Philadelphia. They had come to the gallery in search of an unusual wedding present for the grandchild of one of Sophia's friends. The stunning young woman, probably not more than twenty and dressed entirely in black with stark makeup and jewelry, stood bewildered behind the counter. She did not quite know how to interpret Sophia's tears. She looked apologetic, dismayed, and fragile. In a near whisper Lauren explained that her mother had lost her husband recently. The woman nodded only slightly, but with an expression of relief that softened her artificial face.

Lauren was afraid that on this day of appointments and errands Sophia was about to lose another of these expensive earrings. She had already had to have one replaced. Lauren also wondered why she was wearing such fancy earrings with her fleece vest and warm-up outfit. Shouldn't they be saved for special occasions and worn with a dress? Maybe Sophia wanted to enjoy them now, or, perhaps, display them as a sign of affluence. She was the daughter of small shopkeepers who had worked hard in their neighborhood grocery store. They had come to the United States as poor children escaping anti-Semitism in Europe. During the Depression their grocery store fed their entire extended family.

"We always had food," Sophia had said many times, with a certain air of superiority. She was indeed proud of her past and of her family's role in providing for their poor relatives. They even took people in when necessary. Still, she had to fight with her father to attend college rather than go out to work. Solomon, whose own father had died when Solomon was sixteen, had become the caretaker of his mother and younger brother at this tender age. He had also struggled financially to complete college. Both Solomon and Sophia had successfully moved out of the working class to become college-educated professionals. Sophia even went back to get a master's degree as an adult. Solomon, like Sophia, had taught at the high school level. Right after college he had a very prosperous business for a while, lost the business to a greedy partner, and then worked as an engineer and consultant. But the technology surpassed him, and in his later years he experienced sporadic employment. Sophia and Solomon were proud of their success and especially of their children, who had both acquired advanced professional degrees.

Now it was time to make one last visit to the city house that Sophia had managed to clean out. That is, after several months of painstaking and lonely effort, the house was ready to put on the market. Solomon's piano and his model railroad trains were gone. Sophia had sold them. Gone also were everyone's college books and papers that had been stored in the large attic: Sophia's and

Solomon's, those of their children, and even those of their son-in-law. All of Solomon's political writings had been stored there as well. Apparently, he had been quite prolific during college. Decades of clothes, housewares, furniture, and school projects had been ruthlessly discarded. Now the house was empty.

Solomon had drawn the architectural plans for the house and supervised its construction. It is a large, sprawling ranch-style house of the best materials: brick, stone, and wood. It sits on a spacious corner lot on a quiet street. Lauren remembers having been proud to bring friends to its beautiful grounds. In spring the magnolia and dogwood trees produced breathtaking flowers. Inside, a raised stone hearth gave the huge living room a sense of warmth and opulence, especially since the ebony Steinway piano sat prominently next to it. When the power went out during a blizzard in the 1950s, the family slept in front of this fireplace—lined up, four in a row. At the time of its building, the house was on a frontier of sorts, in a sparsely populated area far away from the dense urban neighborhoods where Solomon and Sophia grew up. A cousin of Solomon's had warned that they would not be able to buy a good Jewish rye there.

On this last visit, though, the sprawling ranch house looked shabby. Inside, the wall-to-wall carpet that had once looked so plush was worn and dirty. Impressions of piano legs and heavy furniture had left their marks. Only a few stray items were left in the house—some old lamps, an ironing board, a watering can, some folding tables, and a few old telephones. The rug in Lauren's childhood bedroom still looked remarkably good.

"We took it from Grandmom's house on Thirteenth Street. Every time you threw up on it as a baby we would clean it with vinegar," Sophia reminisced. "They don't make rugs like that anymore."

At first Lauren could not believe that her parents would have taken a rug that had been so abused and put it in their brand-new house. Then she began to see that it made sense at the time. They were a young couple with a young family. Sophia had never owned her own house. Solomon was in a struggling business. Frugality had always been the watchword of Sophia's life.

Without trying, Lauren began to remember her childhood in that house: the dish towel that hung on a kitchen drawer handle. When Sophia reached for it, Lauren and her brother fled to the safety of their bedrooms. They knew they had done something very wrong, and although Sophia never hit them with it, they didn't want to give her a chance. Dinners had sat in the oven waiting for Solomon to come home from work in the small electronics firm he had built from scratch, just like the house. The model railroad trains that occupied half of the full basement provided a wonderful escape from his business worries. Lauren remembered the countless hours she and her brother spent building bridges with Solomon and testing whether the locomotives— big ones such as Lionel and American Flyer—would be too heavy for them. The electric transformers groaned as the trains produced sparks against the metal tracks. Kids in the neighborhood all gravitated to that basement, where Solomon took such joy in their various projects: not just bridges, but also houses, gas stations, and bodies of water. They loved building this whole fantasy world. When the children got tired of model railroading, they would roller skate around the central heating system, barely missing the laundry machines at times. Solomon didn't mind the noise at all; he would always stay with the projects, tinkering for hours with endless patience.

Penelope and Herbert still live next door in their modest white house that Lauren remembered as a strange place to be. The dog, a beautiful, large collie named Ringer for the white ring around his neck, always seemed to receive more attention than the children. Herbert was compulsive about his lawn and seemed to spend entire weekends manicuring it. Penelope was always in the kitchen creating something elaborate and delicious, like homemade hamburger rolls for birthday parties. As a home economics teacher, she was a professional who taught Lauren to sew. She repeatedly described their own daughter as "a disappointment." At the age of forty-five, the daughter was morbidly obese and jobless. Her parents supported her. She died at age forty-six, probably from a stroke.

Across the street lived Lauren's best childhood friend, Darcy. The family owned a wholesale drug business and a yacht along the seashore. Darcy's mother was a Girl Scout leader with bleached blond hair. Her brother, who never could succeed in school, drove a Corvette. In the fifties they would jitterbug to Dick Clark's American Bandstand. Darcy's mother died before she reached the age of sixty and Sophia always said that it was from all the chemicals in her hair coloring. Darcy's house has had several owners, but it's also for sale again.

Sophia's whole life as a wife and mother seemed to be marching out of the city house that day. She even grabbed her three suitcases and asked if they would fit in Lauren's car. She was indeed going on a trip, if only to the summer house that had never had the solidity or the grandeur of the city house. Stepping out of that house for the last time was a step down. Even though she had no need for such a large house, she had remarked several times in the last few months that she did not have to sell the city house for financial reasons. She had worked in the public school system first as a teacher and then as a counselor and had a very good pension. Her exit from the city house really marked the beginning of her life as a widow, not an easy transition.

This once highly desirable neighborhood was experiencing a serious decline in property values. Houses that might have sold for $300,000 or $400,000 four years earlier were now priced at $150,000 or less. The city was encroaching, or so the real estate agents claimed. People with $300,000 to spend were moving further and further north, out to what was once considered remote farm country. Sophia was having a difficult time understanding why her home would not bring a handsome price. She blamed the real estate agents for not appreciating the finer features of the house. She still fantasized about finding an agent who liked the house as much as she did, and who, according to Sophia's emotionally based logic, would get a good price for it. But the combination of location and age—the 1950s kitchen and bathrooms—was rendering the house a liability to be rid of as quickly as possible.

Lauren loaded her car with the last essentials and was ready to relax and do some shopping or at least have some coffee. But Sophia was spent, physically and emotionally; they headed straight for the island and have not returned since that day.

EPILOGUE

The following spring, at the request of the real estate agent, Lauren returned to the city house. The agent wanted a member of the family to see the improvements she had arranged prior to its marketing. Lauren's husband and son came along to inspect the work. As they drove up to the entrance, Lauren saw that tall weeds had taken over Sophia's flower beds. She used to take such pride in arranging the plantings. As they approached the front door, Lauren could see that the once intact flagstone on the sunny front patio was cracked and sunken. A few bright yellow pansies had come up on their own in the curved brick flower boxes that edged the patio, but they were being smothered by some rectangular planters that someone had thrown haphazardly on top of them. The pansies looked abandoned, small colorful symbols of the abundant flowers in beds that had always been mulched and tended.

Inside, the familiar rooms looked distressed. Their former warm colors had been bleached white, but the white paint did not seem to cover the deep opaque colors underneath. In Lauren's old room her childhood mirror was still on the wall; only the rug from Thirteenth Street was gone. The floor was wood all right, but it was so dirty, as was her bathroom. Sophia would have been horrified by such filth! It was a very good thing that she was not there.

The agent opened the master bedroom closet to reveal the old flowered wallpaper. "It would have cost a fortune to paint this too!"

"This is appalling. How odd," Lauren thought to herself. The room was painted stark white and the closet had dark, flowered wallpaper.

But the worst came as they entered the formerly bright and cheery kitchen. The bright yellow, custom-made wood cabinets had been painted a brick color, presumably to match the real brick wall in the kitchen that backed up to the living room fireplace. Lauren remembered the perfectly shined copper pots that used to hang there, and she could still see them reflecting the wonderful textures of the purposely uneven bricks. But instead of matching the brick, the newly painted cabinets seemed to be making fun of the whole kitchen, especially since the floor was still yellow and brown linoleum. The old gray Formica counters and white appliances looked even older and more dated. Nothing in the kitchen matched.

"It's sad," said Lauren's husband sympathetically. She appreciated his familiar sensitivity even more than usual.

"This must be hard for you," her son almost whispered. He had a knack for reading her emotions.

"It is."

PART

Class Imagination and the Creativity of Class

II

Imagination, talents for design, poems, and names reflect aspects of class culture that round out, in a holistic sense, the essential human qualities of working-class culture. Humor, resiliency, and sarcasm are all embodied in creative expression. In fact, it would be easy to argue that creativity is the watchword of working-class culture, the major survival strategy that works on many levels.

The artifacts, actual creations of class culture, have stories behind them that are tied to the identities of both the artifact producers and the artifact receivers. Many of the artifacts are gifts. Included in these creative and expressive elements of working-class culture are talents and sensitivities that mix a flair for design and expression with a kind of cultural sophistication. By examining expressive culture we see a side of class culture and identity that otherwise remains hidden and unrecognized.

The first story in this section I call "Class Artifacts." It begins with the question: What is an artifact?[1] It then talks about the problematics of artifacts and then asks: How do artifacts document class culture? Artifacts are cultural creations; they are therefore also *class* creations. These creations are numerous and varied. They involve a range of things and kinds of things, from folk sculptures to recycled and redecorated objects, to trinkets and models.

All artifacts, regardless of form, must be understood in their cultural context as commentaries on community, power, and the dynamics of materialism. Many of the artifacts are quite ingenious, clever, and beautiful as well. In keeping with common practices of gift giving in working-class communities, the artifacts that function as gifts are not costly, but they are rich in meaning. They carry strong messages.

The second piece is a story that elaborates many of the themes in "Class Artifacts." It is entitled "Interior Decoration," and it describes the artistic talents, sensitivity, and generosity of a group of working-class mainlanders as they help a well-to-do island family to recreate a home for a widow after the sudden death of her husband. The acts of rearranging, repositioning, recycling, and using only the resources that are readily available turn out to have high therapeutic value. It is the hallmark of working-class culture.

"City Lines," the last story in this section, is about the creative strategies developed by working-class community people for coping with the power plays and insults of the representatives of the hegemonic system. The creative use of humor, especially the timing of clever remarks, is one strategy. Being persistently prepared is another. The eloquence that flows when experienced and clever leaders speak from the heart is still another.

"Artifacts belong to dead cultures; they're dull, dull, dull," repeats Cindy with determination. "Who cares about old potsherds and arrowheads? Skeletons I can maybe understand, but vases, and pieces of broken stuff? How can people spend so much time looking for them, anyway? It's a rich people's sport. We common people can't afford those indulgences."

Cindy is an activist—a woman with purpose, struggling for her own identity and place in the world. For her, artifacts have nothing to do with living people struggling with real problems. At forty-five, she is working hard on her bachelor's degree at night, raising a young child, and working by day as a community organizer, a rather vaguely defined job that is supposed to involve projects in the neighborhood—everything from housing to the arts to individual therapy. It certainly isn't clear to her, but she does not want to be overwhelmed, and she takes advantage of being supervised sporadically and from afar by an extremely benevolent boss who always looks on the bright side of things. Often she conveniently says she is out in the neighborhood, or that she is at home sick, but nobody can ever locate her. She spends little time in her office and, on some days, doesn't even pick up her messages. She hardly bothers with paper, much less with the artifacts such as books, memorabilia, and photographs that are so important in the community.

But for Gina and Robbie, the real but unofficial community organizers, artifacts—objects, some tiny, others larger and more imposing, and many in between—mean a great deal. Artifacts provide the social glue, the goods that flow to keep communities intact and individuals mentally compensated. Robbie has spent years fashioning artifacts, and so has Gina. Both women, both grandmothers, pride themselves on creating objects out of nothing—old milk jugs, containers of various sorts, pipe cleaners, fabric remnants. They use artifacts, living artifacts of their own creating and their own choosing, for community work.

"Tell me what you think are the most precious artifacts," Cindy challenges Robbie.

"Those that talk about people."

"What do you mean?"

"You know, a doll or something that sends a message."

"What sort of message?"

"I don't know. Any message that's important to a person's life. Maybe something about their children, their actions, something they really want, something about their past. I don't know."

EASTER BUNNIES

"What are you doing with all of those cotton balls?" asks Cindy as Robbie presides over her kitchen table like a CEO at an annual board meeting.

"Making bunnies," says Robbie calmly.

"Bunnies? What do you mean? We were supposed to be at a meeting a half hour ago. Did you type the minutes?"

"Yes, of course. Hold on a minute. I want to finish this one bunny."

Every year, Robbie fashions Easter bunnies out of plastic milk containers covered with cotton and decorated with images that symbolize aspects of the person to whom she is giving the bunny. She has been known to present each child in her granddaughter's homeroom class with an individualized bunny. Some are baseball players, some soccer; some are dressed in snowsuits, others in bathing suits for those on the swim team. The detailing is extraordinary on all of them; some of the images, which she embeds in the fluffy cotton, are so tiny and hidden on the figure, that it is necessary to turn the bunny around and view it from different angles in order to find the tiny artifacts embedded in the larger ones. One bunny, for example, has a cap and gown, complete with a V-shaped collar made of gold ribbon. Initials sit in the V. A tiny diploma made of tissue paper lies glued into the pink cotton gown. It too has a gold ribbon carefully tied to secure the diploma. The body of the rabbit is white cotton. The cap is made of pink felt with a tassel, fashioned with beige yarn and knotted perfectly, stapled to the top and draped nonchalantly over one side. Pipe cleaners hold up the ears. The overall effect is a combination of humor and seriousness.

Cindy stares at the pink image.

"Why did you make that?" she demands in a kind of huffy tone, implying, but not saying outright, that she thinks such frivolousness is a waste of time.

"For fun," says Robbie calmly and with the usual twinkle in her eye that makes you realize, if you know Robbie well, that she thinks Cindy is way too full of herself.

"Who'd you make it for?" demanded Cindy.

"For a professor I know."

"What do you mean?"

"You heard me, for a professor I know."

"*You* know a professor?"

"Yeah, I do."

"Wouldn't he be insulted by a pink bunny?"

"Of course not! The professor's a she! Ha! Caught you in some male chauvinism!"

"I didn't mean that."

"Yeah, you did. Are all of your professors men at the university?"

"Most of them are."

Cindy shifts the conversation to another one of the bunnies. "What's this bunny here? Why is it so green?"

"It's for Doris."

Cindy scrutinizes the carefully fashioned figure more closely. "What's with the military stuff? Why the army hat and epaulets? Will you look at those boots?"

Robbie knows that Cindy is a pacifist. She's adamantly against all government and military organizations. She's also an anarchist and an atheist, and she doesn't mind imposing her views on anyone who will listen. Robbie is waiting for Cindy to pick up the green bunny and toss it in the Dumpster. But Cindy sits thoughtfully for a while, and Robbie can see the lightbulbs beginning to go off.

"Did you make this for someone?" she asks quite timidly, very timidly for Cindy, who rarely acknowledges that she might be even the slightest bit in the dark.

"It's both for and about someone," says Robbie so softly that Cindy can barely hear her.

"What?"

"I said it's both for and about someone," says Robbie, this time slightly more loudly.

"Who the hell is the general?"

Cindy has noticed that on the front of the green bunny, on the chest, is "The General," written in bold letters.

"Think about it," says Robbie snidely.

A knowing look comes over Cindy's face. She smiles. Robbie explains, "Doris doesn't like being called 'the general' because it points to her bossiness. I've worked with her time and time again. She hands me all the work she doesn't want to do. I do it. Then she accuses me of taking over, or taking credit."

Cindy backs down. "I get it," she says with some timidity.

Robbie and Doris indeed have had "words" on many occasions, some publicly in meetings chaired by one or the other. Robbie has also been made to feel like Doris's lackey; that is, Robbie feels that Doris will only accept her as a subordinate person who is willing to do the work of an organization, not as an equal decision maker and community leader. Competition between grassroots leaders is extremely common, and alliances can shift with the slightest provocation.

The bunny is both a symbol of one-upmanship, an "I got you this time," message, and an indication of affection and respect. It takes four or five hours to create one of these bunnies. Robbie admires Doris for her perseverance and her skills as a strong woman. Doris has overcome many obstacles in her life—an alcoholic husband, race and gender discrimination, single parenthood. She knows how to keep institutions going and works hard. That Robbie is critical of her bossiness is not surprising; it is based on Robbie's own discomfort with hierarchy and disdain for Doris's patience with the power structure.

Robbie considers herself a radical and is perceived by others as such. She often says: "Whatever it takes," meaning, I will do whatever is necessary to get things done. Robbie knows how to manipulate the power structure to the advantage of her community. She is articulate, outspoken, and confident. When she gets angry, she worries about "going off"; that is, losing her temper and saying something she might regret. Even when she "goes off," she is rational and straightforward, and she is often congratulated by people in power for her honesty. "The general" is a symbol of power after all, and Robbie is less willing than Doris to "play by the rules" of those in power. By constructing a "bunny," in the image of a powerful figure, Robbie is engaging in criticism not so much of Doris but of the power structure itself. She's creating a "living" artifact that works as a counter-hegemonic tool.

"Let me show you this one," says Robbie abruptly, clearly wanting to change the subject.

"Oh boy, here we go with religion!"

"Not really."

"Who's that one for?"

"Megan."

"Megan?"

"She's Mr. James Strong's wife."

"Why is it so small?"

"Have you ever seen Megan? She's small enough to be a large child."

"Really? How long have you known her?"

"All my life."

"I understand the cross means she's probably Catholic, right?"

"You're catching on."

"What's this dark brown stuff? It's all smudged and nasty looking."

"Oh, that. That's for all the shit she has had to take all her life."

"Very funny. What kind of shit, exactly?"

"Oh, all sorts, everything from having to fix meals for twelve every night, to watching grandbabies, to dealing with some of her children giving her grief about her spending their inheritance. Think about it. What right do they have to be counting her money in the first place? She should spend that money before they both pass away. They need to go on the riverboats when they can. You can't take it with you."

Robbie identifies with Megan because she is the wife of an elder community leader. She is, in the most positive sense, the woman who has stood by her family in all of the struggles to maintain and revitalize their community on the river. Whenever she can, she attends meetings and hearings. She is her husband's support and his companion as well as a participant in her own right. Their home is the keystone of the community. It's the place where anyone in the community, family member or not, would feel comfortable coming for help, advice, or simply a safe place to be.

One winter, when it was unusually dreary along the river bottoms, neighborhood teenagers left their own artifacts and icons in the city-owned and -managed recreation center. They painted windows with flower boxes and curtains on the walls of the ceramic room; they smashed ceramic pots so that potsherds lay scattered on the shelves where vases and figurines had been waiting to be fired. They reconfigured the ecology of the rec center when ceilings collapsed from plugged-up sinks. The weight of the water was too much for the structure to bear. The kids were angry at "the recreation" for its rigid rules and authoritarian staff members. One day when it was raining "buckets," a young City Recreation Department employee would not allow a group of teenagers into the center early to play basketball. One boy, a kid with a long family history in the community, even volunteered to take responsibility. It was a war of wills and generations—powerful against powerless.

In reaction to the "vandalism," as the city authorities saw it, the Department of Recreation closed the neighborhood center for over a month. Megan's home became the place for teenagers to go for several months. They fixed things, helped her out, ran errands, looked after younger children. She cooked for them and gave them money for fast food when she was too tired to prepare meals. Many of the kids were her own grandchildren.

A HOME MUSEUM

Cindy gets up from the table and looks around on the bookshelves. She sees that Robbie's collection of artifacts is not restricted to bunnies. Small sculptures stand ready to be admired. Cindy's eyes fall on a ceramic horse.

"Did you make this at the rec center?"

"Oh, a long time ago. It's nothing special." Cindy looks more closely at the horse and sees that it's the merry-go-round kind with a pole coming out of its back. It's playful, painted mostly white, with pink and mint-green decorations. She knows Robbie well enough to know that for her it's a symbol of a very special part of her personality—her love for children and her ability to relate to them as genuine, real people. At times she jokes and calls herself Peter Pan, the person who never wants to grow up. In her everyday life, her special care for the children of the neighborhood has been demonstrated over and over again, sometimes in very small and playful ways, such as her fashioning of Easter Bunnies; other times in gigantic, life-changing steps, such as her informal adoption of a child of drug-addicted parents.

The merry-go-round horse is really a toy, a specially selected one that also represents the ups and downs of her life. The fact that it can be thought to move up and down and around at the same time is important, Cindy thinks, for she often reflects on the high and low points of her own circuitous life.

MUSHROOM BASKETS

Mushrooms sometimes come in large, three-pound wooden baskets with wire handles and flat wooden lids that are almost ovals, really rounded off rectangles that sit covering some of the largest and whitest mushrooms imaginable. Special blue paper protects them from bruising, almost as though each one is too precious to touch with human hands. Most people would throw away these baskets. Not Gina. She seizes every opportunity to decorate, embellish, and transform.

"Don't even think about throwing those baskets away," she warned Lauren, a friend from childhood. "I'll use it for something." Lauren knew she was serious and started stockpiling the baskets in a closet. One day Gina appeared with an extraordinary-looking object in her hands. It was a mushroom basket covered with red and white pleated fabric. A large red velvet ribbon stood perched on the handle.

"I don't believe it! It doesn't look at all like a mushroom basket," said Lauren.

Mushroom baskets are not the only things Gina has transformed. Everything in her house is decorated in the most minute detail. She takes old pillows, old furniture, and old objects and makes them beautiful—recycling, she calls it. Her kitchen is "rooster city," she says. Everything has a rooster on it: pillows, tablecloths, platters, cookie jars, towels. The colors are magnificent. Her husband also loves artifacts of various sorts. He's a real collector, especially of clowns. He displays them in the kitchen on a shelf of the china cabinet next to a framed picture of their two-year-old granddaughter. Gina says, "She has cheeks that don't quit." There are large clowns and small clowns, cloth ones and ceramic ones, musical ones and silent ones. One of the small clowns plays "Oh What a Wonderful World"; another plays "Here Come the Clowns." They're cheery and beautifully arranged. They are next to Gina and Vinnie's wedding portrait. He's wearing a white suit with white leather boots. She's wearing a long bridal gown with a train and is holding a beautiful bouquet of yellow roses. She looks like an angel. He still has the boots.

Gina takes great pride in her abilities to transform things—to make ordinary things extraordinary, to see beauty and humor in the most difficult and, often, ugly of circumstances. Gina spends a lot of time in the spiritual world of liturgy and prayer; she attends Mass daily. Transforming the profane into the sacred is a profession for her. Her church parish is her community. She cares for people by providing work and camaraderie—humor to order. Her crews of housecleaners don't just clean; they alter space with improvements that matter. Dolly makes beds as though she were about to tuck in her dearest grandchild. The corners never come out of their perfectly configured places. She arranges pillowcases like she is getting ready for an interior design exhibit, with the greatest artistry—wonderful color combinations—greens with rich blues, whites with pastels. She and Joe, her husband of many years, work together—placing things just right, folding and smoothing. Joe sings as he works—arias from *Aida* and *Madame Butterfly*. It's a pleasure to watch and listen.

Gina has inspired them. She translates her philosophy of beautification into all aspects of her life, whether she is creating new artifacts or reinventing old ones. She talks about giving the ugliest and dirtiest of objects her TLC—tender loving care. A cliché. Maybe. But Gina is sincere. Her husband, who she says "can't sit still," waters his plants. She says, "The plants are happy for their drink." There's a spiritual quality to her voice. It's almost as though she had private communications with the supreme being. Even when she is incapacitated with an inflamed shoulder from overuse, she is calm and smiling. She jokes about Vinnie bathing her and enjoying it.

Gina has been through rough times and talks about a time when she didn't know where the next dime was coming from to feed her small children. She takes the power of prayer seriously. But she also has a wonderful sense of humor. When she spends a week cleaning houses in the midst of a ninety-degree heat wave, she talks about spending time in a sauna.

Interior Decoration

Lauren's father, Solomon, died suddenly on July 17, 1997—leaving her parents' cottage a worn museum of family artifacts. Almost fifty years of summers had seen four generations in that small cozy house. Grandma Rose spent many sunny days sitting on the porch reading while Sophia organized the household and made sure everyone was comfortable. She worked constantly, but no one seemed to notice.

In the 1950s, three-bedroom cottages at the seashore were affordable to many people, especially on the bay side of the island. Schoolteachers, artists, and musicians of humble means could spend summers in this undiscovered, remote place. The cottage was spacious and airy, with wonderful cross-breezes and a southern exposure that captured sun and warmth even in the midst of winter. The tributary that led out to the open bay protected the little house from wind and storms—perfect for keeping the family's expanding collection of tiny boats. When the land's west wind brought biting black flies and chilly ocean waters to the island's beaches, boating, swimming, and fishing by the bayside lagoon were always attractive options. As the children grew older, they became experienced sailors who prided themselves in being able to tack in and out of the narrow lagoon. Motors were taboo. The bay water was reliable, a steady warm temperature all summer and into October. This was a bit of local knowledge, common sense, actually, that islanders always cherished.

Cousins, some very distant cousins, on both Sophia's and Solomon's sides of the family, would bring their friends and line up sleeping bags on the living room floor. The house seemed to be infinitely expandable. Years before, their parents rented summer places further south along the shore, but they never bought. This house was theirs. As a child Lauren would watch her older cousins put on their makeup before going out to hear music at one of the local bars. They seemed to always come with friends, and Lauren remembers wanting to be older so she could go with them.

In the thirties, Solomon and his younger brother, Martin, worked their way through college playing jazz in these same establishments. Solomon would talk about musicians smoking marijuana and thinking that their playing had reached extraordinary heights, when, in fact, they were playing wrong notes and off key. Martin always looked skeptical about the anti-drug messages. He and pot had always had some familiarity. He visited regularly, though, both before and after he had a family, and he would always play music. The kids adored his immature ways. The summer before he died he came to that summer house just to see it and the family one last time. He talked about the precarious state of his health. He died that fall of a pulmonary embolism.

The house has a kind of sturdiness to it. It has survived the storms that threaten the island regularly. During the three-day nor'easters that bring rain and cold winds in summer, the kids played Monopoly and baked chocolate chip cookies in the kitchen, which had a large knotty pine picnic table with wooden benches. If you sat on the end of the bench it became a see-saw, so if you liked someone, you would warn that person to sit toward the middle of the bench; if you didn't, the naïve person would end up on the floor with, and many times without, a cookie. The house even survived the '62 storm that swept so many larger and fancier oceanfront houses into the sea. "It's the lagoon," Lauren's mother, Sophia, would say. This canal in back of the house did, in fact, send the water out to the bay and keep it away from the house.

The family knew that a storm would be serious when they saw Gregg, a seasoned islander and fisherman, put the cover on his boat. In his twenties, he was the handsome captain of the lifeguards; in his thirties and forties, a dashing football coach. His family spent summers on the island for many generations; he married one of the twin daughters of the household across the way. She was from a wealthy Main Line family without pretensions. Gregg wooed his bride by spending hours fishing with her father in an old flat-nosed garvey. Waves in the lagoon meant high tides and strong winds. Most of the time it was very calm, a large, natural swimming pool right in the back yard. The children learned to swim there and taught younger neighbor children as they came along.

After Solomon's death, Lauren had arranged for Gina and her crew of housecleaners to help excavate the cottage. Layers of stuff had piled up in closets and in bedroom corners. Open packages of food—the cookies and candies that Solomon loved so well—had been sitting for what seemed like years in the kitchen cupboards. She knew Gina's warmth and humor would be welcome at this difficult time. Lauren's brother, Alan, and his wife, Marlene, were there to share the work and the decision making. They had flown in from the West Coast and were staying only a few days. Their busy law practices could be abandoned temporarily at a time like this, but their own life seemed to have a course of its own.

Gina, herself quite small, took one glance at Marlene's anorexic-looking body and ordered, "You—you need to eat!"

Including Gina's two helpers, Roberta, Gina's closest friend and neighbor, and Marian, a seamstress struggling to make a living and member of the church parish, there were six people poised to begin the project. Roberta and Marian dispersed to the kitchen and master bedroom. They could see that there was much work to be done and they were eager to begin.

Sophia was receiving condolences from close friends at Lauren's house. There was to be no funeral. Sophia believed that grief and mourning were private, personal matters. Besides, she was exhausted. Her daily treks to the hospital with Solomon to have his blood checked had consumed her. She had to abandon her normally meticulous housekeeping, which was, under normal circumstances, very difficult because Solomon kept absolutely everything. She had to let things go in the house. They never could seem to get his levels of blood thinner right, and her anxiety caused her to hover over him constantly. At times she looked so tired it was difficult to tell which one was the patient.

Gina paused and stood with hands on hips in the center of the large open living area. She had that special quality of sympathy and objectivity, having known the family for years. For her the household objects did not hold memories. As both an insider and an outsider, she could step back, survey the situation, and think clearly about rearranging things.

"What do you think about moving the brown sofa over there?" Gina suggested tentatively. "That piece of furniture—it's lovely. What's it doing hiding in the corner? Let's move it where people can see it."

The piece was a grainy wooden antique secretary with shelves and a fold-out writing desk. Lauren and her husband had purchased it almost thirty years before and deposited it there for safekeeping. As young, nomadic professionals, they did not want to move it from place to place. Parents do inherit from children on occasion.

Marlene and Lauren began to think about rearranging the furniture. Lauren was torn—ambivalent. Part of her wanted to keep the house the way it had always been. Another part of her said that it was time for change. The change shouldn't be too radical, though. It couldn't be. There wasn't time.

Marlene stood by in neutral. As Sophia's daughter-in-law she really didn't want to take a position. Lauren could feel the pressure to get things done, though—to decide on some plan of action. She wanted to focus on the tasks. But she wanted to start small—with chairs, not couches. Solomon's brown leather recliner really did not need to be in the same old place. It simply looked too empty. Neither did the TV—its huge screen had dominated the room for the previous five years. Sophia had been angry when he spent so much money for it. "What do we need it for?" she screamed after not being consulted on this rather major purchase.

Why should the TV be the center of attention in the new version of the summer cottage? Solomon had spent a lot of time in that chair, eyes fixed on the news, the O. J. Simpson trial, about which he knew every detail. The chair had footrests, but even when his legs were swelling, he often didn't use them; he was stubborn that way, especially when Sophia would nag him. To keep the chair and the television in their original places would only accentuate his absence for Sophia and for the family. It was Sophia's house now, and she preferred the privacy of her bedroom when she watched her programs late at night. That way, when she fell asleep while watching, which she always did, she would already be in her bed.

The kitchen seemed to be an easy place to start. Solomon had spent a lot of time there, preparing his breakfasts and lunches especially. He would arrange his food carefully on his plate and then proceed to eat slowly. Sophia would often prepare food too, but she would do it quickly and eat in large mouthfuls, in order to get on with her chores—laundry, housework—and her exercise—her walks at the lighthouse pier and her swim in the lagoon. Solomon was never one for moving his body. He liked to sit and he liked to eat. He was pensive, often with a furrowed brow that was difficult to figure out. Was he tired, annoyed or angry, hungry, frustrated with life in general, or was he just thinking? He had a fabulous memory for detail in many areas. He knew every current event in depth, almost as though he had memorized each day's *New York Times*.

His worn pillow was still on the white plastic chair at the head of the kitchen table. After consulting with Lauren and Marlene, Gina took out the old white plastic kitchen chairs and replaced them with some ladderbacks that had for years been laden with junk in the master bedroom. They threw away Solomon's worn old pillow. They knew they couldn't erase him, but such reminders of his age and infirmity did not seem necessary to keep. Ironically, he died in his favorite place, collapsing in front of the refrigerator. Lauren's last memories of him envision the paramedics bending over him on the kitchen floor.

Even in her somewhat numb state, Lauren kept telling herself over and over: "We can't erase him, nor do we want to try. Memories are important. But we can try to ease the pain of his abrupt departure." Gina seemed to have a great deal of wisdom about her state, and seemed to understand exactly without having to exchange any words on the subject.

Six years before his death, Solomon had suffered a stroke that left him with shuffling feet and real difficulty with balance. Right after the stroke his speech was slightly slurred, but his mind was very much intact. Within a year his speech returned to normal. The stroke had been caused, in part, by sleep apnea. He was Pickwickian—that is, he would fall asleep at the breakfast table because he was not sleeping well at night. Of course, when Lauren or Sophia, his wife, would wake him up, he would deny that he had been asleep.

"I'm just resting my eyes," he would protest, many times angrily.

Lauren knew quite well that Solomon had a sleep disorder and tried to convince him to seek help. But denial was one of Solomon's greatest strengths. It was only after his stroke that he acknowledged his sleep problem. He was given a machine to sleep with that would help him breathe, and he used it, part-time. It was very awkward and uncomfortable though, and the equipment often sat, unused, by his bedside. His "sleeping machine," as Lauren called it, became another of his many things to dispose of from the house. Alan would take it to the hospital for someone else to use.

Three years before his death, Solomon had been diagnosed with congestive heart failure. He was on blood thinners and diuretics. A month before he died his legs swelled up like balloons—severe edema, they call it in the medical profession. Ulcerated sores oozed fluid from his lower leg. Lauren was worried then, so much so that she bought him a special chair and footstool so that he could keep his feet up comfortably. She also had to beg him to sit down. Gina nagged him too, in a teasing way. "I wish I could sit there in the shade."

"Too much of a good thing," he'd reply and conveniently neglect to put his feet up.

"Feet up!" Gina would order.

"Come on, Daddy," Lauren would coax.

He was a short man, five foot two and shrinking. He was very stocky, and it seemed to hurt him to put his feet up, but he would obey Gina without frowning. She had a strong, definitive, but light touch.

Easing Sophia's pain became a team effort as Gina, Roberta, and Marian worked with the bereaved children. Six people worked for three whole days, taking turns to make sure that Sophia was not left by herself to receive the many friends who came to offer condolences.

Amazing amounts of stuff were crammed into that small summer house. It had always been the repository of comfy old clothes—those too ragged, faded, torn, or baggy to wear in the city. Boxes full of old clothes came out of the overflowing closets. There was even an old quilted garment bag in the master bedroom loaded with still more old clothes. But how many old clothes does one family need—even an extended family with lots of guests?

Marlene and Lauren began to go through the women's clothes—this after Marlene and Alan, Lauren's brother and her husband, had put all of Solomon's stuff in bags for Gina to take to family, friends, neighbors, the hospital, and the church. It was quite a relief to have the stuff taken away.

Lauren and Marlene piled the remaining clothing on Solomon's leather recliner and sorted the pieces, one by one. Memories lived in those clothes. Some were from Lauren's college days, long gone now since her children are now in college. She was surprised and somewhat confused by Marlene's patience and willingness to help, but she was grateful at the same time. In-laws have always been somewhat mysterious to Lauren, unpredictable. Behind Marlene's somewhat cold exterior is a soft heart.

"We should have done this ten years ago," Alan remarked several times.

"But what would have been our incentive? How could we barge into the house and start throwing things away?"

Lauren was right. It takes a crisis to clean out an old house. There were some amazing finds. Domestic archaeology, one might call it. A package of cupcake papers marked with a price of ten cents. Old glasses, books, jewelry, Solomon's many medicines.

Somehow, Gina knew all the right tasks, the right actions. Her empathy, her sensitivity to the needs of the family was startling to Lauren, even though she had known Gina since childhood. It wasn't what she said, it was what she did, really what the cleaning crew did. It all seemed so natural, so easy, so unforced.

Gina and Roberta took on the kitchen with vigor. They didn't just clean it; they curated it—exhibiting what needed exhibiting. They displayed the handmade pottery on open shelves, for example. They stored what needed storing—grains, cereals, jellies. Solomon was a real collector of foods. Even Lauren was disoriented when she tried to find a glass. But this was good, she thought. It's a new kitchen.

From Gina: "How about a new cloth for the kitchen table?" "Excellent idea." Somewhat guiltily, Lauren took off for the nearest variety store. No time for Wal-Mart or Kmart now. Lauren hated these superstores anyway. They were simply too big and too time-consuming both to get there and to find things. Lauren had always valued time over the few cents saved. There was a small, compact store on the northern end of the island that had been there for years. It carried everything from housewares to bathing suits. She would be able to return quickly. Everyone else was still cleaning and moving furniture. She came back with two flowered oilcloths—just the right accent for the new "old" kitchen. They were colorful and easy to clean with a quick wipe. They would appeal to Sophia's practical sense without adding to her self-created mountains of laundry. She never wore anything twice and could not stand one item of dirty clothing in the house. A tablecloth that required washing would have been a burden.

The transformation of the kitchen was remarkable. The colors in the oilcloth even matched the bowl of plums they had retained for continuity. Everyone likes a bowl of fruit on a kitchen table.

The living room was more difficult, with its three couches, lots of clutter, and a feeling of just too much stuff in one room. Gina and the children placed Solomon's leather recliner in the corner by the never-used front door. A television corner came into being with the addition of a sofa and some tables. The rest of the furniture fell into place, including a sitting area looking out onto the lagoon. As Gina figured it, since the house is on a lagoon, why not be able to look at the water? Logical, of course, but no one in the family had ever thought of it. This put two of the sofas back to back and divided the large room nicely. Deliberation about the coffee and end tables seemed endless as they kept moving them from place to place. Gina kept deferring to Lauren, and Lauren, emotionally spent from the shock of the previous few days, kept wanting someone else to make the decisions. She was not the kind of person who cared very much about the details of interiors in the first place, having never devoted much time to homemaking. Lauren kept turning from Gina to Marlene, who remained neutral. Alan seemed preoccupied with going through his father's things and didn't seem to want to participate in the interior decorating. That left Gina.

Gina decided to place the lovely antique secretary as the focal point of the dining room, with the table angled out from the corner for easy access and serving. They moved the cupboard that held the dishes to the wall opposite the kitchen, in a much better position to display two large and intricately sculptured covered dishes. The transformation was incredible—all because of Gina's imagination.

Lauren's son, Noah, pronounced the transformation "awesome."

But Gina was still anxious. Was it her place to make these suggestions? She knew Lauren well, but this was not Lauren's house anymore. Sophia had always had a kind of uneasiness with Gina that she could not quite put her finger on. She seemed to like Gina well enough and had always been friendly and warm to her and her family. But there was a gap between the families, and Gina always felt it. The subtle overtones of condescension— the *we are more successful than your family*—came through to Gina loud and clear.

The changes made in her house were certainly well beyond the realm of cleaning. Would Sophia like all of the changes? Or, would she feel that her home had been invaded and somehow violated? Were there too many changes? Were they too drastic? They had thrown out a lot of things. Would Sophia miss them? They didn't want her to see the house until everything was completed. Gina feared that Sophia would criticize a small detail or that she would be upset and think that something was out of place when Gina had not yet found a place for a memory-filled object.

Gina's relief when Lauren told her that Sophia was delighted with all of the changes seemed to radiate throughout the whole community. Sophia loved the cleanliness and the absence of clutter. She had fought clutter all of her married life, fifty-four years. She also liked the addition of color and light.

"I have a new house!" she exclaimed. "Everyone in mourning should have this done for them!"

EPILOGUE

It is now two years since Solomon died and the house came under the hand of Gina's interior decoration. Sophia has not moved a stick of furniture or a piece of pottery. Everything is just as Gina left it. Every year Gina does Sophia's spring cleaning and admires her handiwork proudly.

Sophia has accomplished some improvements. She has had the kitchen floors redone by the best floor company in the area. They are now wood floors that match those in the rest of the house. At Alan's request, she has purchased a light and ceiling fan to replace the old lamp over the dining room table. Sophia refers to Gina as her decorator.

The chambers of the City Council are darkly paneled. Enormous, ornate chandeliers hang mostly unnoticed from the high ceilings. They nevertheless have a strong presence as they shed a yellow haze over the cavernous room that has multiple doors—glass ones at the back entrance under the balcony and some hidden wooden side doors for staff. In the midst of hearings, citizens slip out through the back to have private conversations in the hallway or in the offices that line the dark corridors. The real work gets done in whispers and behind closed doors.

The spaces in council chambers are divided, clearly and unequivocally. Perhaps *stratified* is a more appropriate description, as lines are carefully drawn. The mayor and councilmembers sit on raised platforms facing the audience, women in conservative gray suits, men in jackets and ties. One elderly woman councilmember sleeps with her white head down. She's been on the council for so long, no one objects to her dozing. In fact, they have come to expect her naps. She's highly respected among the liberal establishment as an advocate for communities of poor and disenfranchised people. The atmosphere is always somber and serious—intimidating. You can feel the weight of the issues. Councilmembers might as well be wearing wigs and robes.

A person testifying before council stands in front of the audience as a supplicant, that is, at ground level looking up at

councilmembers. City staff members sit off to the side, antici-
pating every document, memo, and needed piece of information. They never sit for very long. The side doors open and close
constantly as staff members run from chambers to their offices
to return with folded pieces of paper to hand to their bosses.
The meetings are videotaped and broadcast repeatedly over City
Cable, a local public TV station. It's relatively easy to keep up
with City Council proceedings, that is, if you have the time.
One elderly man in the community stays tuned to City Cable
for many hours of each day and keeps a running tab of the votes.
His wife is a prominent community leader who often testifies
before council.

Private citizens wishing to speak before council must sign
up in advance and be sure to keep to the allotted time of three
minutes, no longer. The clerk of council, who also sits on the
raised platforms, calls the time to the precise second—maybe
earlier if he thinks the person is not worthy of speaking. He
sizes people up—estimates their power, their clout, their respectability. How he does it is mysterious, but he seems to have
a measuring system based on some vague set of criteria: past
experience, age, gender, race, dress. Some community leaders
dress up to go to City Hall; others wear everyday working-class
clothes—jeans, sweats, T-shirts—so as to remain authentic to
themselves and to the community.

In order to reach council chambers on the third floor of the
imposing brick building that is City Hall, a person must first
walk up the worn marble stairs. They are steep and slippery,
imposing and polished. There's a dip in the center of each step
from years of feet trudging up and down. City Hall's elevator is
very small, takes forever to come, and when it does, it creaks
and rattles and complains so much that it seems to be saying,
"You shouldn't be here." Once one reaches the third floor, the
walk to the chambers feels endless, like it is almost an entire
city block. Elder community leaders, whose years of manual
work have taken their toll on muscles and bones, struggle to get
to hearings. Doris worked for a wealthy white family all her life.

She's retired now, almost eighty, and a prominent member of her church and her community. Eileen, some fifteen years younger than Doris, has had many jobs, most of which did not even begin to touch her rich talents. She's fought many battles, personal and political. Doris and Eileen are a formidable team. They always arrive at hearings breathless and sweating, summer and winter. Doris came as chair of a hard-working and long-standing community board. She presides over her board by insisting that everyone hug her before they sit down. "Never give up" is her motto. "We are persistent," she'll say at every board meeting. "We persist." Eileen was there as chair of another neighborhood organization. "We should have left all this warm stuff at home," they lament as they take off coats, hats, and gloves.

A citizens' advisory group. Every city, large or small, has at least one, usually several. Often they're social clubs that do nothing but meet endlessly. People like to hear themselves talk, especially rich and powerful people. They go on and on at length, posturing, lecturing, sometimes for half an hour or more. This one thought it was different, though. It cared. It cared about preserving community. It had a social conscience. After all, it had members touting long histories of civic action, with all of the proper connections throughout the city—corporate connections, mostly.

I had never seen a citizens' group in action before. I confess that I quite naïvely thought them to be superfluous and beside the point—meetings for people who had a lot of time on their hands but who did not accomplish a great deal. Citizenship always had a stodgy ring to it. The word reminded me of boring lessons to memorize and textbooks with pictures of the American flag and the Statue of Liberty in color. It seemed like a concept out of the past.

Meetings of this citizens' advisory group took place in a large committee room, around a huge, heavy, wooden conference table. The chairperson, a thin, very proper looking, gray-haired white male with a soft voice and a controlling manner, presided at the head of the table. When he looked at you with his icy blue eyes, he needed to say very little. The conference table seemed to me to be much more intimidating than the raised platform in council chambers. There was no escaping from full view. Everyone could be seen and heard from every angle. Even a small movement—a scratching of the head or squirming in the chair—was closely scrutinized and recorded by those around the table. At the first meeting I tried to retreat—*hide* is more accurate—among the seats on the periphery of the table, but I was soon beckoned to the table itself. I guess it seemed standoffish of me to want to sit separately, but in truth, I was uncomfortable with the tensions, real and imagined. I couldn't tell the difference.

For morning meetings, some of which began at 8:00 A.M., the community leaders, Doris and Eileen among them, all had white bags with coffee and sweet rolls from the bakery on the corner opposite City Hall. This establishment was part of a string of well-liked old-time German bakeries that had been making bread and sweets since the beginning of the century. The white bags crinkled and crunched as napkins were retrieved and crumbs spilled onto the floor from the wonderful-looking Danish and cinnamon buns. The three-piece-suited citizens stared and looked annoyed, but the crumpled, half-awake city staffpeople didn't notice, or if they did, they kept their eyes on their ceramic coffee stained mugs that seemed all of a sudden to demand immediate attention sitting next to their Filofaxes, yellow tablets, and newly sharpened pencils.

"Community input" is a favorite phrase among citizen elites, but it is never certain that they understand what it means. The citizens' advisory board said they wanted community input, but they clearly didn't want the accompaniments. They wanted something abstract and comfortable. Perhaps they liked the idea of community participation, but not the reality. Comfortable to them meant quiet, clean, and neat—compliant. Not noisy bakery bags and crumbs—not coffee that might spill all over their papers, or worse, their expensive clothes. They certainly didn't want community members who said too much, either.

One petite red-headed woman, whose stylish wool, short-skirted suit fit her just perfectly, leaned over to me and whispered, "I eat my breakfast at home." She was an older woman with grown children, so at first I thought she had forgotten what it was like to get up and ready children and grandchildren for work and school before readying oneself for an early morning meeting. Her suit looked like she had just purchased it in the Armani section of the elegant, Fifth Avenue Bergdorf Goodman on a recent theater weekend in New York. She and her husband were always taking trips that involved culturally enriching experiences. They particularly liked archaeological ruins in Mexico and had recently returned from an expedition to the Yucatán Peninsula where the Mayan pyramids were spectacular. They talked about being absolutely fascinated by such an old culture—how its richness and longevity were unbelievable—on and on.

I'm sure it wasn't easy for corporate wives to sit around a table and talk to community people with yearly household incomes equivalent to what they paid their gardeners in one month. The differences on the surface were, of course, very marked, but even more dramatic were the cultural gaps separating rich and poor. But maybe the elites viewed local poor communities with the same distance they used to view the Mayan pyramids. And that was precisely the problem.

Neither was it easy for the community people to put up with the elite power games, many of which happened nonverbally or on the phone after normal business hours. One community leader complained to me that her comments never appeared in the meeting's minutes, which were taken by a student from the university's school of planning. Somehow that student had a map of the city's power structure in his head, and he only recorded what the map indicated as points of interest.

I remember one particularly fiery woman on the citizens' advisory group, the wife of a prominent physician in the city. She had jet-black hair (dyed, of course), beautiful textured-tweed clothes in extraordinary colors, and a very aggressive but patronizing approach to people of lesser means. She had a way of asking questions whose answers were either obvious or painful, or both, and she did so without addressing people directly. "Do you think we could gather some information on that?" she would ask, looking around the room. Sometimes her eyes would fix on the chair; sometimes she would glare at a community leader. "How about a survey?"

Everybody knew the needlessness of a survey documenting traffic problems in the community—everybody, that is, except the citizen elites. Traffic was life-threateningly horrible on the main thoroughfare through the neighborhood. After all, it took people from the eastern suburbs to downtown. To commuters it was a pass-through—almost a superhighway, if the speeds of fifty to sixty miles per hour are any indication—not a neighborhood street. Best to stay off the street at rush hour, since no one obeyed the thirty-five-mile-per-hour speed limit. There were no cops to pull people over, as they were just five or so miles east in a wealthy neighborhood. "There they stopped people going thirty-two in a twenty-five." Did Miss Black Hair ever experience what it was like to stand on a street corner with a five-year-old waiting for the school bus in the dark?

One day, as a meeting was dragging endlessly on, a neighborhood leader leaned over to me and whispered, "Do you think she needs a hand down from her pedestal?" I was astonished that such creative humor could be mustered at a time of utter frustration for community leaders. Perhaps she had been encouraged by the powerful poem Eileen had written about traffic on the community's main street. It was an impassioned piece, written as only someone who had spent all of her life in the neighborhood could.

A few years later at a City Hall hearing, in the same council chambers, Miss Black Hair came over to show me a text she had written for Doris, the elderly neighborhood leader with long years of experience at City Hall. "Do you think it is okay for me to give this to her to say? I think this is really important," she said, after making a trip to the other end of council chambers to find me. This was progress, I thought to myself. A few years ago, she wouldn't have thought to ask. I quickly recovered from the shock of her thoughtfulness, though.

"Well, if you think it's so important, why don't *you* get up and say it?" I suggested.

She thought for a moment. "But . . . but, I want to give it to her."

I wanted to ask her why she felt it necessary to put her words in other people's mouths. But I did not. I wanted to tell her that Doris was quite capable, if not more capable than she, of getting her own message to the powers that be. I just said very quietly, but forcefully, "*You* should say those words; they're yours; if you want to get your message heard, you should deliver it yourself."

Just after I spoke to her, Doris rose and gave her own speech from the heart, complete with the appropriate visual aid, a photograph she carries in her purse. Her eloquence would have been difficult to match on the floor of the U.S. Senate.

PART

Class Vulnerability

III

Class vulnerability is complicated and multilayered. It refers to possibilities and susceptibilities that may be hidden for a long time, but that can surface very quickly and without warning to the vulnerable person. The possibility of criticism is one form of vulnerability; susceptibility to attack and injury—physical, cultural, and psychological—is another.

The power structure regards working-class people as dangerous, not as being in danger. But from the inside, there are many felt dangers, imaginary and real. Class vulnerability is difficult to write about precisely because it is so subtle.

The first story, "Rehab," is about a kind of vulnerability that comes with too much commitment to family and community. James Strong can overcome physical illness, but he cannot conquer the depression he feels seeing his community sold off to developers. He feels a deep sense of loss, as though a family member were passing away. His commitment to the community makes him vulnerable. A strength turns into a weakness.

In "Bridal Shower," the vulnerability that results from abuse does not belong to the working class alone. Rather, it takes many forms and is masked by different class cultures. In this story, Celia's history of abuse is shrouded in respectability, even luxury. She is the daughter of a physician and is married and has a child. She looks healthy and well groomed, except that she has asthma and she smokes, a form of self-abuse. The bride, Sarah, is the victim of several forms of abuse, including that of her own class status. Maintaining the cultural forms that mask genuine feelings and obviate authenticity brings about an epiphany for the bride.

"No Legal Claim" is about an extended family of urban-to-rural migrants who are struggling to adapt to life in a small rural town. It contains a complexity of overlapping class issues—class boundaries, class crossing, class identity—but the main issue is the vulnerability of class itself when class identity is ambiguous, that is, when an adolescent is not sure where she belongs classwise.

Sally's low self-esteem stems from her mother, Paula's, low self-image and prior abuse by Sally's father. Role confusion between mother and daughter and father and uncle (mother's brother) further lowers Sally's level of security and in turn raises her mother's level of anxiety when Sally takes unreasonable risks, as she does when she allows drug users to ride in her car. She does this both because she is a kind soul and because she craves attention and friendship. She is picked up by the police, handcuffed, and thrown in the back of a police car. She is nervous, but the police interpret her nervousness as a cover-up, as lying.

Paula has no legal claim on her daughter's father or on his property just as Paula's brother, by hegemonic standards the most successful person in the family, has no legal claim to Sally. This situation is itself ambiguous and is only exacerbated by the fact that Sally's father is slowly dying from multiple sclerosis.

Dropping out of school is another issue in "No Legal Claim." While leaving school is complicated socially, psychologically, and economically, it is becoming increasingly common. Sally cannot tolerate school. She tries half school, half home schooling, and that works for a while, but then she stops going to school and gives up home schooling altogether. Like many working-class adolescents, she decides she will take the GED exam.

Rehab

A white-haired woman labors with her walker down the polished linoleum hallway. Her face is lined and straining. The hallway seems endless, its slippery floor yet another obstacle to overcome on the path to recovery. But recovery for what? is the question. Periodically, a young head—an aide, a nurse, a son, a daughter—peeks out of a doorway to check on her progress, if you can call it that. It's slow, at best. She breathes with difficulty from her already sunken chest. Her eyes are glassy as they try to focus simultaneously on the floor and the tunnel-like hallway.

Holy Trinity Hospital rehab unit. It's a new facility with all of the latest technology for helping people to recover from serious, debilitating illnesses. The equipment—pulleys, handles, weights—is all very shiny, so shiny it screams at the struggling, elderly patients to try harder as they strain to lift themselves out of hospital beds and bathtubs. The new patient lounge, with its large varnished table, refrigerator, and microwave, looks like an upscale conference room, or a lunchroom in a workplace where the management cares about its employees. It's used by nurses and visitors, but rarely by patients.

James Strong is recovering from surgery for compressed vertebrae in his spine. He isn't yet able to negotiate the slippery hallway, even with a walker. He can barely make it to and from the bathroom. He's a seventy-eight-year-old activist and community leader who has spent his whole life living and working in the community. Even after the loss of sixty-one pounds, he is still a very large and imposing man. He's over six feet tall, and though he bends as he uses the walker, his color is good and his blue eyes are sparkling. The pain he had been living with for so long appears to be gone; but, as his wife points out when he complains of his slow recovery, it took him forty years to develop the pain, so he should not expect his recovery to be instant. He is still short of breath.

He and his wife, "Megan," as he calls her, are grandfather and grandmother to dozens of children in the community, only some of whom are related to them by blood or marriage. They've lived in this close-knit river community since the 1940s when James owned a very successful boat hauling business. In the 1950s his dock even had a seaplane base attached to it. He and Megan's brother, Clem, who used to take his boat to work downtown, had a special affection for this beautiful and often dangerously powerful river. They spent many evenings and weekends sitting on their favorite bench watching and listening to its sounds and movements, the barges and boats that go up and down past back yards. They would talk about the height of the river and wonder when it was next going to flood.

During big floods, the river can cross the east-west thoroughfare that bisects the community and parallels the river. When basements fill with water, community members rally together. Water pumps, kerosene stoves, and helpers appear as if out of nowhere. Neighbors help neighbors, and since many neighbors are kin, the distinction between family and neighbor becomes blurrier than usual. Bags of mud emerge from basements. The bearers of these bags begin to look like mud figures themselves, so covered are they. When the river does get to a certain height, perhaps just short of flood level, James's sons join others in a boat-sinking ritual. "If the boats are on the bottom we know for sure where they are." The river is an intrinsic part of every person in the community. "We are river people—river rats," the locals say. An outsider dare not use this term.

The river belongs to the community, but in ways that outsiders do not understand. It's for every community member to use and enjoy, to see, smell, touch, and identify with. People hear certain barges and riverboats and know what time it is. If it's property, it's everyone's property held, at least symbolically, in common. In the spring, community children come out for the river sweep with rakes, garden gloves, and huge garbage bags. It's a community cleanup project, but more than that, it's a rite of solidarity; it's a chance for adults to teach children how to handle the river—to deal with its danger as well as to think about its meaning. In the last flood, James's children made him sit on the sidelines; they feared his back might give out if he tried to stand too long or carry anything heavy. Here was a man who was used to leading the efforts to combat the river; he knew its dangers intimately; he was not used to watching others work. He became depressed.

Over the course of forty years, the Strong clan has established a substantial homestead in the midsection of the community, the section closest to the city's downtown. The homestead is a lot like the family compounds in the country, only there is a busy street running through it and a river behind it. Their son, Mark, and his family live in the house next door, and two of their daughters live in houses across the street on the river side. The houses, all within shouting distance, are compact, with porches across the front and kitchens in back. In spring and summer, James spends a lot of time on the porch. It's his out-door living room. People wave and honk to him as they go up and down the street. A niece lives in a small apartment building just to the north. For several years the building was closed. It's finally been redone as affordable rental housing through a com-bination of city and private (corporate) monies. James and Megan attended many community meetings to fight for this affordable housing that now occupies prime riverfront property. The rich people don't like this housing at all. They think the poor have no right to see the river. River views are getting ever more scarce and expensive.

Another daughter lives in an adjacent community that is quite close to her old neighborhood. When floods get too bad, James and Megan leave reluctantly. They will sleep at this daughter's house and then insist on being driven back home to spend each day. Home is important. It's familiar, comfortable, and safe. James feels he must stay in touch with activities in the neighborhood; so must Megan. She's the reference point for many children, including her own grandchildren, who check in with her after school.

Outsiders think the community is a dangerous and crime-ridden place, but they don't really know the perils experienced daily by community people. Neither do outsiders understand the river or the community the way residents do. One of James's granddaughters went to the "boat school," a very successful trade school situated on a barge on the river. Teenagers learned how to work the river barges. They became licensed; they received certificates; they found jobs. The school worked for community kids. One of James's many granddaughters wanted to be a boat captain, and one of her aunts had already begun to call her "Cap" for short. The whole family was proud. But the school board closed the school before she could graduate, ostensibly because of lack of funds, but actually, as one seasoned community organizer put it, "because it was working too well for poor children. Whenever high-risk children are well served by a school, the system shuts it down."

In their room in the rehab unit, Megan sleeps upright on the brown vinyl loveseat next to James's bed. It's that old kind of vinyl that's very shiny and rubbery. It looks really uncomfortable. She holds his hand all night for fear that he will try to get up and go to the bathroom by himself. She's really worried that he'll fall. She looks exhausted, but she cheers up as his newest daughter-in-law, Robbie, and Lauren, an old friend of the family's who is the same age as James's oldest daughter, come into the room. Megan is as small as James is large. She's well under five feet tall, but her presence fills the room.

James's lunch tray arrives. It looks really bland and institutional. He rejects the cold spaghetti even after Robbie takes it twice to the microwave in the patient lounge to try to warm it up. He plays with the food, twirling it on his fork, pushing it around the bowl. It's almost as though he were trying to transform the thin red sauce into something more succulent and hearty. He seems hungry, but the food really is unappealing. He doesn't touch the pile of dead-looking lettuce leaves. He eats only the chocolate pudding in slow, deliberate spoonfuls with a slightly shaky hand.

Lauren looks on with sadness. She remembers all of those times around his dining room table—happy times with grandchildren running in and out to check on grandma and grandpa. James always sat in the same place, on the right-hand side of the table as you came in the door. He never sat at the head to preside, but somehow he clearly was in charge, in his own way. "Grandpa," everyone called him, including his five daughters. Megan always bustled around him, running in and out of the kitchen making tea and coffee in the back of the house. He would sit there at the dining room table for hours, offering advice and counsel to family, friends, and neighbors. You could count on him being there. Megan made sure there was lots of food on the table and in pots in the large kitchen. She was always offering people snacks and drinks, coffee, tea, or pop. At various times of the afternoon, grown daughters and nieces appeared with prepared food in covered pots and dishes. Some of his grown children had just awakened from sleep after working third shift. Others were getting ready to go to work or just coming home. Oyster stew and macaroni and cheese—favorites for Lent.

Suddenly Lauren remembers that she has fruit in her backpack. "I have a pear and a navel orange in my backpack. Would you like it?"

"I'll try an orange," he says, brightening up a bit.

Megan stands by his side and peels it patiently. She does it mostly by feel since her eyesight is very bad. When she reads, she peers through a small magnifying glass. She likes to read the obituaries to see whether she knows anyone and needs to attend a funeral. It takes her almost all day to read the paper. As she proceeds to break the orange into bite-size segments and hand them to him one by one, he smiles and looks very content. He eats with relish.

Lauren looks around the room; her eye lands on a full fruit basket from the community council sitting uneaten on a shelf in the corner. It's quite large and contains a variety of fruits, including oranges and pears.

"He won't touch the fruit because it's from 'them,'" Robbie explains. "Them" refers to the developers and land bankers who have taken over the community council in his neighborhood and who are in the process of buying out the community for profit. They pay lip service to caring about the community, but basically, James sees them as self-interested and greedy.

James Strong is a man of principle; he will not eat from the hand that is constantly grabbing the neighborhood—people who have systematically tried to destroy the community, a community James has worked to preserve and revitalize for most of his adult life. The large addition on the recreation center building would not have come into being without his efforts. He fought persistently, in meeting after meeting. City Hall's Department of Recreation has always been reluctant to give money to poor communities, but James is a very persistent man. He has never been known to give up in all of his years of fighting City Hall. His name appears on community development plans from the 1970s, and he is a founding member of the neighborhood development corporation and heritage center. He has spent countless hours in highly contentious meetings, hearings, and other gatherings in and outside of the community. During these tedious and aggravating sessions, he would sit back in his chair and listen intently, saying little. When he did speak, his words were barely above a whisper, and a hush would come over the room. People strained to hear him, for what he had to say was worth listening to by community people and outsiders alike. He embodied the sentiments of the community, but he was never confrontational or hostile. There were times that the situation warranted strong stances and strong language. James always remained calm. Outsiders viewed him as weak, but community people didn't. His restrained style signified control and strength. Community elders never "go off."

After he eats the orange he wants to know what is going on in the neighborhood. He asks repeatedly for updates and information about the meetings of the various nonprofit organizations and about the new people who have taken over the community council. He wants to know their occupations and their motives. He checks people out carefully, this time from a hospital room.

A few months before his hospitalization, one of "them" hurled an insult at James. A developer called him a redneck and proceeded to refer condescendingly to community residents as "you people." In keeping with his style of restraint, James never answered back; he refused to stoop to their level. Instead, he resisted with silence. This incident so provoked his new daughter-in-law, Robbie, that she agreed to have her name written in on the ballot for the executive board of the community council. Before the insult, Robbie had resolved to stay away from the executive board of the developer-dominated community council. She had served her time on the board and had herself been the target of insults and worse. But nothing mobilizes grassroots daughters more quickly than insults to elders.

James is home from the hospital now, depressed, tired, and feeling useless. His independence has been squelched by the doctor's prohibiting him from driving. Worse than that, he has learned that some of his brother-in-law Clem's property has been sold to developers, including Clem's house, a charming old structure, right on the river.

"I don't like just sitting around," he laments as he rocks back and forth on an overstuffed rocking chair in a dark corner of the living room. His large body sinks into the chair's stuffing and makes him appear smaller than usual. It is odd to see him separated from his dining room table where he sat so upright. In fact, no one is in the dining room on this day. When Robbie's nephew comes in to ask her if she could watch his children, he looks surprised and a bit worried as he sees the emptiness of the table.

The living room is cozy, but dark. One of the great-grandchildren, Erin, plays with a mechanical Easter bunny that says "Tickle me" when you lift its paw. James laughs at the ridiculousness of the bunny, and, of course, by the attention everyone is giving him when he manages to get it to work. Erin is proud that she has taught "Grampa" something, and her face beams with accomplishment. Erin's mother interrupts the fun, though, when she stops by to take her to afternoon kindergarten. She's on her lunch break from her job in the advertising department of a large, multinational corporation. Unlike most East Enders, she's had a few years of college, and that, combined with her natural smarts, has allowed her to advance in the company. Recently, she's been asked to travel to other cities to set up advertising systems for branch offices. In fact, she's very much in demand. "That's how good she is," says Robbie proudly of her adopted daughter. Robbie takes care of her granddaughters, ages eleven and seven. Four generations in one room.

Against the wall a large old couch sits with a soft cotton afghan draped over its back, just waiting to cover a tired child. Megan says it's Angela's favorite place to sleep. She's another great-grandchild who used to live in the upstairs apartment of Grandma's house before her mother, Mim, moved in to live with Robbie in a nearby community. Now Mim must move back into her parents' house to help care for her father. Megan is simply too small and too old to handle his large bulk and his mood swings.

James's other grown children, Mim's siblings, live nearby, but they seem to have their own lives and cannot be relied upon for his daily, ongoing care. Some have made it clear that they resent having their inheritance spent on expensive, rehabilitative care. Mim and Robbie, however, have encouraged James and Megan to spend whatever is necessary for their comfort and well-being. Robbie has really become part of the family; she has become a parental figure in Angela's life, and although she is reluctant to give up her own apartment, she will move in with Mim and Angela. Robbie is not sure how Megan feels about this arrangement, but James seems comfortable with it. He understands how valuable Robbie has become to Mim and Angela.

Since Angela suffers from both epilepsy and depression, her health requires close monitoring. It seems that every time Angela spends a weekend with her father, Mim's ex-husband, she "takes several giant steps backward" and has to be reevaluated both medically and psychologically. She has trouble concentrating on schoolwork and tends to act out in class. Her family rejects the diagnosis of attention deficit disorder, but she is on Ritalin nonetheless, along with several other medications. Robbie's high intelligence and sophisticated approach to both educational and medical bureaucracies is enormously helpful to Mim, who is often intimidated by red tape and class discrimination. Robbie watches closely Angela's reactions to the different medications, and she is not afraid to negotiate with health care professionals on Angela's behalf.

Bob, a close friend of the family and longtime East Ender himself, advises James to buy "the girls," Mim and Robbie, a small house that has become available nearby in the community. It's on the block Robbie used to live on when her mother was still alive, and it's about five blocks from James and Megan's house. They need to be close to James and Megan, and they need to be back in the community. Bob and James have been friends for over fifty years. They have worked together as founders of the neighborhood development corporation and have been leaders in community affairs. They understand the dynamics of large extended families. Over the years in summer, Bob's houseboat goes upriver to the "camp," a lot on the river on which James and Megan have a mobile home. The two families have cherished their time together.

James loves the outdoors. He yearns to go to the "camp," once it is fixed from flood damage. In the meantime he likes to go for rides into Kentucky along the river and into the country. Mim and Robbie spend many evenings driving him around. Once he is in the car, it takes a great effort just to get him out. One night he fell asleep and several people were required to get him into the house. Of course, Megan stayed with him and she fell asleep too.

He resists the indoors. On a recent trip for ice cream he took his ice cream out to the car, claiming that it was too hot inside the old ice cream parlor with the Tiffany lamps and homemade ice cream and candy. It was. He went through two sundaes that day and enjoyed every spoonful.

Lately James has been staying in bed on the first floor of the house. Some days he doesn't even get dressed. When he is depressed he won't sit in the living room or at the dining room table.

EPILOGUE

Robbie is now spearheading a community charter school planned to be located in a wonderful old stone building on the river, right across the street from James and Megan's house. Robbie has been through many of the same struggles that James endured as a young adult: slow and recalcitrant bureaucracies, specialized and obtuse vocabularies for saying simple things, delays and stumbling blocks, city politics and power plays. But James has been her inspiration. When things get so rough that the obstacles seem insurmountable, she spends an afternoon at the dining room table.

Class
Vulnerability

A small upscale restaurant in suburbia—selected for its trendiness—the perfect place for a bridal shower. A vegetarian menu, fresh strawberries in winter, servers dressed in black, and a touch of art deco surround tables set with cloth napkins, white tablecloths, and fresh flowers in delicate, glass vases. Judy, mother of Sarah, the bride, knows a discount florist. She's had the cake specially made by a private caterer who is a friend of a friend. Judy has attended to every detail, right down to the white chocolate party favors. She's the kind of person who has a contact for just about anything. She buys nothing retail.

This December day is very dreary—gray with a mixture of wet snow and rain. The young friends of the bride trample in wearing long flowered skirts, chenille sweaters, and boots. Warm woolen clothing might have been more practical, but style prevails; they seem to be pretending it's spring. Exquisitely wrapped presents pile up on low shelves underneath a large bay window in the front of the restaurant. A modern-day dowry.

Sarah, the bride to be, is attractive—petite and perky, if rather tense. Sarah's aunt knows that there have been many sources of tension in Sarah's life. In fact, Aunt Lauren remembers one incident in great detail, even though it occurred more than twenty years before the bridal shower. Lauren had been invited to Sarah's house for dinner. She had been hesitant about accepting the dinner invitation since it required her to travel some distance in the middle of winter and in the midst of her very busy schedule. At this time in her life, family obligations did not receive high priority. She had never felt close to Judy, and she had never liked Brian, Judy's second husband and now Sarah's stepfather. To her Brian seemed egotistical, smug, and a self-proclaimed expert on everything. He patronized Lauren as though she were a child not quite deserving the respect of an adult—not quite in the same generation. Lauren's husband, Judy's brother, was out of town when she allowed herself to fulfill a family obligation to visit. That way, he would be spared this time. Lauren was pregnant with their first child, and traveling was getting increasingly difficult. She could barely fit behind the wheel of her small car, and she didn't like the long drive from their apartment in the city to Judy's house in the suburbs. She felt great ambivalence as she parked in front of their rambling old house—relief that she had arrived safely, dread that this would take more time than she could spare. Perhaps she might learn something as a prospective parent, she rationalized.

As Lauren slowly climbed the few stairs to the house, she heard a lot of talking, maybe even arguing, but, feeling relief that she had finally arrived in the cold early evening, she rang the doorbell anyway. Large families are noisy, she told herself. As the door opened, Sarah and June, who were probably seven and six respectively, seized Lauren's hands and led her to the piano bench. They sat close on either side of their aunt like tight bookends and proceeded to show her their latest pieces, the same ones Lauren had played as a child—French folk songs, ballads, and patriotic anthems. They started with some easy duets, but they seemed anxious, even scared. At first, Lauren read their anxiety as excitement, as cries for attention in a large and rather chaotic household. At that point in her life, she was not used to children, and probably would have viewed any household with children as frenzied and out of control.

Just before dinner was served, Lauren learned that Brian had locked his own eldest daughter, Celia, then twelve, in the dark, unfinished basement of their large house. Apparently, she had been down there for some time before Lauren's arrival. It was

not clear exactly how long. Lauren was somewhat afraid to in-
quire about the circumstances, in part because it was not her
place to interfere with the family's disciplinary practices, but
also because she fully expected Celia to be released for dinner.
She wasn't. Instead, they all sat down at the enormous kitchen
table. To Lauren it seemed almost institutional. Before the food
was served, Brian threatened to strap Sarah in her chair if she
didn't stop squirming. Lauren did not see the squirming as problematic, but simply as the normal movements of a young child.
There was something about the way Brian spoke and gestured
that made Lauren afraid that he might strike Sarah or send her
down to the basement as well. The look of fright on that child's
face cannot even be described. Lauren sat at the table helplessly.

She had waited a long time before beginning her family, and she
felt powerless in the face of Brian's almost maniacal rage. He
was a very large man, and Lauren feared for her own safety and
that of her unborn child if she tried to intervene. She did make
herself a promise, though: never would any child of hers be
allowed to spend time in this household unaccompanied by at
least one parent, preferably herself or her husband. Grandparents would not do; they would be powerless in the face of Brian's
unpredictable anger.

A few weeks after her stay in the basement, Celia swallowed
an entire bottle of aspirin. The incident was only one of several
suicide attempts for her. Fortunately, a sensitive guidance counselor helped Celia function and survive in the context of her
Cinderella-like existence, complete with what the system saw
as a wicked stepmother. No one considered that her father might
be the wicked one. Of course, the extended family was kept
completely ignorant of these terrible facts. As June, Sarah's younger
sister and Judy's very attractive second daughter, grew to be a
teenager, she ran around with the wrong crowd. She became
pregnant, had an abortion, and the family kept it quiet. No one
was supposed to know. June's ability to sustain long-term relationships had been seriously, perhaps permanently, impaired.

Sarah's twenty-eight years, stylishly cut dark brown hair, and
her honey-colored eyes now mask her tenseness somewhat. She
plays the role of hostess with aplomb, but with a great deal of

calculation. "This is my sister June, and my other sister Celia and my two young half sisters." Both of the eleven-year-olds, the offspring of Sarah's parents' second marriages, giggle with excitement. The older sisters look expectant. June is also in her late twenties. She's still single. Celia, who is well into her thirties, is very dark, large, and almost matronly. One of the eleven-year-olds looks almost exactly like Celia. They have the same father, and they seem to have inherited his excessive talkativeness. At eleven, Nancy is already taller and older-looking than Sarah. The other eleven-year-old, Linda, daughter of Sarah's father and stepmother, is still demure and childlike in her white blouse, velvet skirt, and Mary Janes. Everyone is trying to smile, but some people are wondering why there are so many sisters. Others are observing the sisterly dynamics while they keep track of people coming in, what people are wearing, and where to stake out a table. Sarah and June are full sisters, but they look nothing alike. Sarah and Celia are stepsisters, and Sarah is the half sister of both young girls, the children of her parents' second marriages. The guests smile as they hug Sarah, who is clearly working hard to manage all of the complicated relationships.

Actually, there are six sisters and one brother from four different marriages. Sarah, June, and Aaron (who is absent until dessert) are from their mother, Judy's, first marriage to Robert, Sarah's birth father. Celia and her younger sister, who has decided to avoid the party entirely, are the daughters from Judy's second husband's first marriage. Robert's second wife, Sarah's stepmother, is there with her own complicated family: a mother and stepmother and numerous categories of sisters. They sit separately at a large table in the back of the restaurant. Robert's mother, Sarah's grandmother, is sitting with her relatives. She looks wonderful. At eighty she is trim and conservatively stylish in her blazer and slacks. She looks very happy and says so as she smiles and greets people. Still another separate table holds the groom's mother and her extended family.

The lone brother, Aaron, once clearly put it this way: "I have two sisters, two stepsisters, and two half sisters." He's a huge, burly guy with long, unruly red hair. You can tell he's June's brother, only he's not neat and fastidious like his sister. He doesn't look anything like Sarah, who resembles her father's side of the family. Most of the time he's a genius at managing his relationships with sisters, although their fights are often vitriolic and long lasting. He struggles with his father and mother, especially his father, who cannot understand his choices and lifestyle. He lives with a divorced woman and young child and spends his time making pottery, not what a doctor's son should be doing. He says his father thinks Sarah is perfect. She went to the right college and is marrying a physician.

Aaron's mother, Judy, a nurse, and father, Robert, a surgeon, were divorced when he was an infant. At that point he had two older sisters, Sarah and June, who were three and four, respectively. Aaron has paid a high price for the angry and conflict-filled relationship between his divorced parents. He was considered to be a slow learner in grammar school, was diagnosed with attention deficit disorder in middle school, and barely made it through high school. Judy refused to put him on Ritalin, however. He never finished college, and his father has never forgiven him for it.

Sophia, a wise older woman and close friend of the family, who is sitting at yet another table, with Judy, remembers the phone call of more than twenty years ago when Judy called tearfully to say that Robert was packing a suitcase and abandoning her with three small children. Sophia was so upset, she sent Solomon, her husband of forty years, to try to convince Robert to stay. It was not just the idea of divorce that upset her—she believed that divorce was evil and the easy way out of solving problems—it was the actuality of the divorce itself and its long-term effects upon children that upset her even more. She was old-fashioned and believed that children need fathers in whole families. Broken families are just that, and they produce broken children with broken lives. But it was too late.

Sophia had been worried for some time that Judy's parents had been too involved in the young couple's lives. They had recently retired, were already quite elderly, and had always practiced very rigid life patterns. Their visits to the young couple's home often lasted weeks. They thought they were helping by taking over Judy's household. Sophia knew, too, how carefully Judy had schemed and manipulated to "catch" this bright young physician. Judy had been raised in a physician's family and was expected, almost from birth, to become a doctor's wife. That was what her nursing degree had been all about.

Robert, though, had always been an independent person. He didn't like coming home from a hard day at the hospital to be told instantly by his mother-in-law that it was time to eat supper. He wanted to relax and eat later. Judy was no help to him. She treated him as a kind of acceptable but inconvenient appendage. She was her parents' daughter first and his wife only secondarily. Once, in a confidential conversation with his sister-in-law several years before the divorce, Robert lamented Judy's dependency on her parents. Robert also knew that, no matter how hard he worked or how successful he became, his in-laws would always look down on him because he had not been born into a physician's family. His mother had worked as a secretary at a prestigious medical school, and his father had run a small business. Moreover, he had a retarded brother; no one pointed out that this brother had been normal at birth but had contracted meningitis at the age of three. Instead, the retarded brother was viewed by Judy's family as only one more example of Robert's family's inferiority.

In 1975, Judy remarried. Brian, also a physician, but more than ten years older than Judy, became the stepfather to her three children, Sarah, June, and Aaron, and Judy became the stepmother to his two girls, Celia and Marsha. After a prolonged illness, Brian's first wife had died of cancer, leaving him with two young, prepubescent daughters. Judy and Brian had been introduced by a bleached-blond friend who was sitting with Judy at one of the smaller tables. Her jewelry alone could have paid for the three-course lunch.

"He needed a wife to take care of those girls," she said. That Judy was desperate for a husband, any respectable husband, was left unstated. Stepdaughter Celia was at their table also but wasn't paying attention to the chatter. Celia had been joined by Aaron's girlfriend, a woman about her age. Celia looked amazingly good, considering her very troubled childhood. As the oldest child of this so-called "blended" family, she had become a little Cinderella at the same time that she was recovering from her own mother's death. As the oldest stepchild, she received the least attention and the most responsibility. On the mantle in Judy and Brian's house are pictures of Judy's biological children. Celia and her sister are nowhere to be seen.

The turbulent past seems to be held in suspension on this celebratory bridal shower day. Celia sits happily at a small table that includes mostly older women. Sarah sits at a large table surrounded by her friends, many from childhood. This shower is for women only. Celia is now in her early thirties and the mother of a three-year-old daughter. Her understanding husband and mother-in-law have nurtured Celia's natural warmth and friendliness, and they've helped provide loving child care for her baby. Serious health problems have, at times, incapacitated her. Her thirtieth birthday found her in the hospital with a life-threatening asthma attack; yet she smokes heavily, as does Aaron's girlfriend, who is sitting next to Celia.

The salads have been sitting at the place settings for some time and have grown limp in the overheated and somewhat overcrowded room. A choice of three different pasta dishes is served, each with an increasingly pretentious description. The plates arrive with huge portions—gluttonous amounts of bland pasta with almost no sauce and few accompaniments.

As lunch is winding down, Celia and Aaron's girlfriend go outside for a smoke. Aunt Lauren gave them her "why you should not smoke" lecture, but they seem totally absorbed in their nicotine addiction. Besides, they are enjoying each other's company as mature women with children and as professional artists. Aaron's girlfriend is a single parent with a four-year-old son. She works full-time, as a stage set designer, as does Celia, who is a print maker.

As Sarah begins to open her gifts, the tables start to loosen up; women sitting in the back of the restaurant move to the front and stand over those seated. The two eleven-year-olds rearrange their chairs to get closer to the opening of presents. They want a front-row seat, even as they play with the fancy chocolate party favors, large and ostentatious white carts with donkeys pulling them. The young girls unselfconsciously devour the sweets, almost as though they hadn't eaten any food that day. Perhaps they think they must eat quickly, before someone takes the candy away. They haven't yet learned to watch their diets. But their childish behavior seems a welcome distraction from the tensions building in the room. Lauren has been watching Judy throughout the party; she is on edge. To be in the same room with her ex–mother-in-law and her ex-husband's new wife is extremely difficult for Judy, especially since all of the work and preparation for the shower fell on her. She still looks worried that something might go wrong, and she is exhausted. Certain people alternately refuse to make eye contact or force smiles.

It is probably better that Judy's mother is not there. As the grandmother to whom Sarah is closest, her absence does not go unnoticed. Several people have asked for her. But there can be no doubt that she would have added to the stress of the gathering. This grandmother had learned to force her smile very early in life. Orphaned at the age of seven, she had been raised by her three wealthy sisters. Family albums include photographs of gala balls at the best New York hotels with the finest in clothing (including elaborate hats), food, and entertainment. Luxury had been an intrinsic part of her childhood and adolescence. Proper behavior was expected. Her more down-to-earth husband used to say that he had three mothers-in-law. If she had come to the shower, this grandmother would have repeated, over and over, insincere exclamations of "Isn't this wonderful!" when in fact she couldn't wait for the whole thing to be over. Her feigned cheerfulness would have made Sarah even more nervous. Her absence, though, is somewhat mysterious, at least on the surface. This is, after all, a bridal shower for her oldest and favorite granddaughter. Is it the wet snow, the presence of Robert's family, her inability to control what might happen, or some combination of all three that has kept her away?

Class
Vulnerability

"It would not have been a good idea for me to go," she would say a few days later, sounding as though she had almost convinced herself that she had been ill.

Food and sex are the most prominent gift themes, although stodgy Waterford crystal lends an air of respectability to the offerings. Skimpy, "intimate" apparel—negligees, underwear—comes from the bride's young friends. The most practical things, if you can call them practical, are appliances such as Cuisinart food processors and pizza-making kits. No young couple should be without these. Not a frying pan among the gifts. A beautiful, hand-thrown and colorfully glazed cookie jar made by Aaron's girlfriend Jackie and given by Aunt Lauren doesn't seem to go with the fancy registered place settings and the Waterford crystal pitchers times three.

The young bride seems to have just the right words for each present, though, almost as if she had consulted a thesaurus and rehearsed various phrases of appreciation in advance. She keeps up the repartee as she carefully and efficiently unwraps each gift, one by one. Her two youngest sisters provide a chorus of oohing and ahhing on cue, with a great deal of repetition and just a hint of sarcasm—the wisdom of children. These two eleven-year-olds know, somehow, that it is absurd for a modern young couple to be burdened with all of these expensive but useless "things."

The matron of honor, who has taken time off from her first year of residency training in surgery to attend the shower, uses a paper plate to make a bonnet out of the ribbons. "That was a lot of work," Lauren comments sympathetically.

"I like to keep busy," is her cheerful response.

"I can see that."

It takes a full two hours to open the presents. The women who had moved to stand in the front of the restaurant remain standing and peering for the duration. There is a kind of snobbish voyeurism here, one that seems to be calculating something not quite tangible. Perhaps theirs are efforts to measure the elaborateness of the gifts, or maybe they are to assess Sarah's level of enthusiasm in her reactions to the presents. Maybe they just want to be thanked. As the last ribbon is placed in the bonnet, Sarah puts the bonnet on her head for a photo; it is indeed beautiful, with magnificent colors lighting up her now tired and lined face. She seems to have aged just in the last few hours.

There is little chance for real conversation at this event, but Lauren does manage to talk a bit with Sarah's sister, June, who has been living in Tennessee for several years teaching elementary school. She has always been very focused on education and is fond of small children.

"My boyfriend is moving across the state for his job," June tells Lauren. "Since I'm not really into the commitment thing, I am looking to meet people. Maybe Sarah and Daniel will move nearby. Best for all of us to get away from the Midwest for a while."

Sarah has come over just in time to hear this last sentence and is nodding her head vigorously. "We need some time to ourselves."

Indeed they do. To save money, Sarah has been spending the last year living with her mother and stepfather. They have a huge house, and Sarah does spend a lot of time with Daniel. Still, it seems incongruous that she would choose to move back home after having her own apartment for several years after college. She certainly knows how independence feels. She also knows how it feels to be pressured to marry. Sarah met Daniel on a blind date arranged by a friend; she had felt some urgency as she had been fast approaching thirty, with no apparent prospects. Perhaps she wanted to be by her mother's side for this precarious year. These days, her stepfather was rarely home. Doctors could certainly affect dedication and spend endless days and nights at the hospital. That theirs was not exactly a model marriage had been clear from the outset. But his absences now make for a house with all that much more peace and quiet. When he does come home, he sleeps.

As the shower ends, the presents are piled into Sarah's future mother-in-law's trunk for storage in her basement. One wonders whether many of them will not permanently reside there. At least it will be safer than Brian's basement.

As they are loading the car, Sarah discovers an unopened present. It is a rather large and somewhat heavy box with very plain wrapping. She stands in the wet snow by the trunk of the car and opens it, looking around to see whether the giver is looking on. But by this time everyone except Sarah's new mother-in-law, who is sitting in the driver's seat, has retreated back into the warmth of the restaurant. The box turns out to be filled with nested pots and pans with no-stick bottoms. The family's housekeeper had signed her name on a small card inside the smallest saucepan. Sarah suddenly realizes that the most practical present of all managed to arrive without notice from a quiet, hardworking woman who was not even invited to be part of the celebration. She stands for a moment in the cold dreariness and feels relief, in part because the whole ordeal is finally over, but also because someone who is very important to her cared enough to deliver these useful items. Just at this moment, her future mother-in-law turns around to ask whether there is a problem.

"Oh no," Sarah replies, with forced cheerfulness. "Thanks so much for keeping these presents for us."

"Don't worry about a thing, dear."

As her mother-in-law drives off, Sarah bursts into tears.

No Legal Claim

I had no legal claim to Turtle.

"No more legal claim than the city dump has on your garbage," I said.

"Her aunt just told me to take her. If it hadn't been me, it would have been the next person to come down the road with an empty seat in the car. I guarantee you, Turtle's relatives don't want her."

"I understand that. But the problem is that you have no legitimate claim. A verbal agreement with a relative isn't good enough."

BARBARA KINGSOLVER, *The Bean Trees*

I had known sixteen-year-old Sally before I met her; in fact, I've known many Sallies, girls who are special—singled out, set apart by themselves and by others as intelligent, sensitive, and energetic in their approach to life—too sensitive and kind for their own good and too burdened by responsibilities and expectations, their own and others'. You can see the depth in her bright blue eyes. You can also see the fragility. Sally is the focal point of her family's attentions. Her milestones, her trials, her accomplishments are a matter of constant discussion among the members of her extended family. They worry when she is ill; they also worry when she is healthy. With the same thick blond hair as her mother, who could easily pass as her older sister, she is attractive, pretty and pleasing, with a certain tough insight and sense of terror that comes from understanding and feeling too much. Her intelligence shows in her face, especially her eyes, and she notices things that most other people miss. She anticipates and analyzes problems that the average person would not even recognize. Her mind is always working.

Sally's mother, Paula, comes from a factory town in the Northeast, home to several generations of working-class people. Sally's grandmother, Vicky, is a widowed seamstress, who, though in her mid-seventies, still sews collars in a factory part-time. Vicky is very talented and can remake and repair garments so expertly that they become almost new. She speaks rapid Polish to her neighborhood friends, having come to the United States as a teenager. Paula's father was a pipe fitter, also Polish. They met at a church social. He worked hard, drank heavily, suffered short-term memory loss, and died in his sixties. Their youngest son, Paula's brother, developed an aneurysm and died at the age of twenty-six, well over twenty years ago. Paula still talks about how much she misses him. His death casts a real darkness over the family.

Until recently, Paula and Sally lived with Paula's older brother, Robby, in the industrial Northeast where they grew up. Paula and Robby have always been very close. It was a land of oil refineries, smoky factories, filthy air, and dense, diverse populations—more and more people cramming themselves into smaller and smaller spaces—spillover from New York City. Sally did well in school, but classes "up north" were large and getting larger—not much chance for individual attention. Not much green space either. In 1991, Paula and Sally left Robby's place "up north" and moved to Breckenridge, a town on the mainland in the rural southern part of the region across from the island where wealthy summer people come to enjoy the ocean beaches and the gorgeous sunsets. Robby stayed. He works for a large multinational corporation in New York. He has access to resources and knowledge foreign to the rest of the family, although it is unclear how far up he will be able to go as someone with an alternative lifestyle. He and his partner, Jeff, are inseparable and often come to visit Paula on weekends. Vicky also lives "up north" right next to Robby. She cooks for him every weeknight. Paula does most of the cooking on weekends, something she does very well.

Paula is very worried about Sally "hanging" with kids who are "not motivated" to better themselves and go on to college. Everyone on the mainland knows what awaits girls who don't finish high school: housecleaning and waitressing. This is a fundamental fact of local knowledge; it may be *the* fundamental.

The house in Breckenridge belongs to Sally's father, Buck, the man for whom Paula is now caretaker. Buck has advanced multiple sclerosis, a progressive neurological disease. He has trouble swallowing and talking. He's incontinent. Often he can't answer the telephone because his fingers won't work. One day he stiffened up so badly, he slid right out of his wheelchair. He has a catheter with a bag.

"Sometimes the tools just don't work," Paula reports. She showers him every other day, unless he has an accident and she needs to "clean him up" several times. "Can't have him smell like urine, you know, like a baby." Paula must lift him in and out of bed and from his wheelchair. Every Wednesday she takes him to the island to see his physical therapist. Getting him in and out of a car is a real chore. He weighs 150 pounds, and even though he's skinny, two people are needed to stand him up and stretch his muscles. Paula worries about getting enough calories into him. Rice pudding and macaroni and cheese are among her specialties. She worries not only about his nutrition, but also about his skin breaking down into bed sores. She buys many different creams. She rarely calls him by his name, though, preferring to refer to Buck as "him." They are not married.

Buck is fifty-four years old, born in 1944. When Paula met him he was a roofer, but he had spent most of his life as a firefighter. Paula lives with him as his caregiver in exchange for his paying the mortgage with his substantial pension. The house is in her name, but she worries that if Buck dies his "other legal family" will go after the house. He has a son in his thirties and is not legally divorced from his wife. Buck rarely sees his "other family," but he talks to his son on the phone rather frequently. His son is constantly asking him for money. Sally has always felt that she competes with his older child for affection and for resources. Buck continues to support his legal wife, a point Paula resents deeply, since they don't even take him for a day's outing and Paula struggles to pay their household's bills. Her legal claim on the house is tenuous. Her legal claim on him is fictional, at best.

Paula is having trouble finding work. At one time, she worked in a pharmacy and became trained as a pharmacist's assistant. She liked the job because it gave her a chance to "use my brain" and it involved helping people. She learned the drugs and their side effects quickly and was happy interacting with the public. The pharmacy is now closed; it was bought by a large multinational corporation and relocated to another state.

On Tuesdays and Thursdays Paula cleans a doctor's office "up north." It's at least a two-hour drive each way if there is no traffic. She enjoys the work, though, and feels close to the other people in the office. They support her efforts to find a better job; she attends their children's weddings and family functions. She combines her work "up north" with visits to her mother and brother, who live nearby. Occasionally, she works in a daycare center, but it pays only $5.05 per hour, and she often finds herself ill from being around so many small children. Sally worries about her mother driving home late and tired on the interstate.

Paula herself needs a gall bladder operation and a hysterectomy. She has had several severe episodes, one that caused her lips to turn white and landed her in the hospital. Her red blood count was so low, it scared her and, especially, Sally. They had to give her ten pints of blood. She has always said she cannot have surgery because there would be no one to lift and care for Buck during her recuperation. Also, she would have to pay out of pocket, since she has no health insurance.

"When I get married, it's Uncle Robby I want to walk me down the aisle." It was Robby who taught Sally how to ride a bike when she was five. It was also Robby who took Sally on a vacation to Florida during her sophomore year of high school when she was being stalked by a fellow student.

"I wanted him (the stalker) dead," said Paula. "I asked God to forgive me for having that thought." Sally had a wonderful time in Florida. When she came back she looked rested—healthy and relaxed. Her school counselor told her so. While Sally was away Paula secretly read Sally's diary and was heartened by her statements about wanting to make something of herself. Sally knows what is expected. Uncle Robby worries a great deal about Sally and Paula, but he has no legal claim.

It's a struggle for Sally to stay in school. She's in her junior year at the regional high school, after spending her sophomore year being schooled at home. It's early in the semester, and Sally has already missed twelve days of school. Paula is very anxious and angry; she says, "It's your funeral."

Jack, Sally's ne'er-do-well friend, is nineteen and is about to return to the eleventh grade.

"You have to be brave to do that. He's classified, you know, as emotionally disturbed. That's one good thing his mother did for him." Sally gives the same speech about Jack that her mother gives to her—all about how he shouldn't throw away his life, how a person must finish high school. Jack is staying at Paula's house once again; without her generosity, he would be homeless. He comes from a family on the island, but they want nothing to do with him. He has been on drugs and has been institutionalized at least once. The last time he disappeared, Paula was very worried. She told him so, despite Sally's warnings not to say anything.

Paula hopes that Sally will go to school now that she has her friend Jack to go with her. But they are giving him a drug test and creating other barriers for him. Sally is depressed; she sleeps a lot, and Paula is worrying more and more. Paula talks about her priorities and about how her first responsibility is to Sally, who has become her life's project. She talks daily with her mother and her brother about Sally's school problems, making it clear that these are their problems as well, even though they have no legal claim.

Sally only feels safe at home. She's really afraid to go to school. Lunch is the most difficult part of the day. The lunchroom is intimidating. No one will sit with her. The other kids call her a "spoiled bitch." They envy her nice clothes, always the latest style, and her caring mother. When Sally is finished with her clothes, Paula sells them at the flea market. Cash is short.

Sally talks about not fitting into the cliques at school. "The kids from the island, Morgantown, and Winston have been at Hopewell since the seventh grade; the kids from Breckenridge came in the ninth, after all of the groups had already been formed." She has the class structure down pat. "Even the honors kids only want to go drinking in the woods on weekend nights. I'd rather stay home and watch TV with my mom. I put my car in the garage on mischief night because I knew they would scratch it. I am worried about driving it senior year."

Paula wants desperately for Sally to succeed, but the more school she misses, the farther behind she gets. Her algebra teacher makes her sit in the back of the room by herself while the other kids are working in groups. "I have no idea what work to do. Last year my geometry teacher helped me a lot. She gave me assignments and deadlines."

Sally has a strong sense of responsibility toward her father, but she feels that the school does not understand her "work" schedule as they do those of others who have paying jobs or responsibilities for younger siblings after school. She pays her car insurance by working long hours in summer—no time for the beach. Sally does not feel spoiled. She feels misplaced and misunderstood.

In many ways Sally is caught between social classes. On the one hand, her family is solidly working class. Breckenridge is a mainland community cut out of the pine forests. They live in a working-class community on a working-class street within a working-class extended family structure. They have working-class jobs. On the other hand, her level of material wants extends way beyond working-class resources, causing jealousy and envy in her immediate community and stress in her family. Her Sweet Sixteen party was held at one of the most upscale restaurants in one of the most expensive sections of the island. In school, though, she is not accepted by people from "the island," either. The fact that she is an "only child" and lives in a world of adults also is difficult. She is a child on the way to adulthood, but she worries about her father and her mother as an adult would. She's in a "special" position "in between." She doesn't have a legal claim to adulthood; neither is she experiencing the joys of youth. She doesn't belong anywhere.

Hopewell Regional High School looks like a prison or, at the very least, a factory. It's an impersonal and sprawling building of red brick, with endless hallways and concrete walls. The office is in the front entryway enclosed by large glass windows. A few display cases contain student-made pottery, but the pots are uninspired, lifeless—a failed attempt to demonstrate that creativity might be possible. The school brings back memories of fear from my own school days—fear of being sent to the principal's office, fear of rigid authority. I stand scarcely three minutes in the central hallway, when someone asks if I have signed in. I simply ask for the location of the cafeteria, where Sally has gone to deliver a message to a friend, and I am offered an escort to the lunch room.

I've promised Sally that I would accompany her to visit Mr. West, a psychologist and guidance counselor. Initially, Sally wanted full-time home schooling, but once she lands in Mr. West's office, she decides to continue at the school. He suggests the 504 program, which would allow her to go a partial day, if needed, and receive five credits for a class in "learning strategies." It would also provide her with the support she needs to keep on top of her classes.

Sally has a very positive conversation with Mr. West, who seems able to tap into all of her concerns, including Jack. He has moved out of Paula's house to his own now that Sally has helped him do something that is acceptable to his parents, namely return to school. Sally tells Jack that she has informed the school that he no longer lives at her address. She is very angry with him for not listening to her. He borrowed money from her to buy clothes and has not yet paid her back. She says she will take the clothes back to the stores. She talks about him as selfish and screwed up.

Mr. West emphasizes how important it is for her to take care of herself, to focus on her life. He also talks candidly about her mother. Sally tells him that her mother is always giving her advice and telling her what to do. He acknowledges that the message her mother is giving her is negative. It says she is not capable of making her own decisions. He tells her she is capable and that the hardest thing for a parent to do is to let go of children. He emphasizes that she must be her own advocate. Once her new program is set up, it can be changed again, and if she doesn't like a certain aspect of her program, she should go to someone in authority.

Sally flirts with Mr. West; she asks him whether his wife bought him his colorful tie. She asks him for gum and he complies, saying in an accommodating tone, "I always have gum." He is very fatherly; he talks about his own daughter, who is in a wheelchair. He talks of her need to play and lead a normal life. Sally is quick; she gets the message about overprotection and its harms.

But Sally is also impulsive; instead of waiting for this new program to be set up, she wants immediately to go see her teachers, that very day. "Bad idea," says Mr. West. "It's only two days before a nine-day school vacation." He is also worried about her impulsiveness, for it could cause her to be slapped or to be ignored if the teachers refuse to go along with this special program that he is proposing.

West calls the guidance counselor, who appears a few minutes later in his office. She knows well the problems of falling behind and explains that this first period is only 20 percent of the total grade for the year. Better to cut your losses, she says, and start afresh in the new period that begins after the school break.

Paula is extremely grateful for the support she has received from friends and family, but anxiety consumes her. She needs some form of therapy—perhaps a well-run group for mothers of "problem" teens or for mothers with disabled husbands, or both. Sally confesses that she worries about her mother at the same time that she depends on her. This role reversal is confusing to Sally.

Sometime during the next week, Sally writes the following note to her mother. It is written on stationery that is nicely designed with a modern angel, complete with a halo, floating horizontally at the top of the page. It is contained in its own beige envelope, with "MOM" written in large cursive letters on the front.

Mom,

> I just wanted to write you a little note to tell you how much I appreciate everything you've done for me. I can't thank you for all the things you've done to help me because I would have to write a book. Mom, you are one of a kind and god may not of given me some of the things that I want but he gave me you. He gave us. You are all that I have and you are the most important thing in my life. And I am sorry for the hard times and the upsetment that I have put you through. But know I am going to do the right thing not only for me but for you to be proud of me. I want you to know that I love you [love symbolized by a heart] and your thoughts and ideas mean a lot to me and have a great impact on my life. You'll always be my best friend, my mom, and the best thing that I've ever had.
>
> Love [another heart] always, Sally

Sally knows that her mother has high expectations for her, but she is afraid she cannot meet them. She knows that this upsets her mother greatly; thus her term "the upsetment." She feels her mother's caring and the power that her mother has over her life. She also feels her mother's anger and disappointment looming over her at all times. She seems to view her mother as a possession, a thing among her many things. The relationships between these things and her self, her sense of self, is not clear to her, especially since her life has come to be dominated by things.

School is out for the week, and unfortunately, it leaves Sally with no structure to her life. She stays out until 2:00 A.M. without calling her mother. Paula is distraught and questioning her ability to cope with anything. She almost crosses the boundary into utter despair.

The car is a major source of anxiety for Paula; Sally has a learner's permit. She is supposed to have a licensed driver with her at all times—someone who has been driving for two years.

She has been taking off by herself, driving aimlessly. Paula is worried about the gas money, too. She's angry and says that Sally will get very little at Christmas, especially since she does not help around the house.

During the vacation week, Paula indulges Sally and her friends. She cooks dinner for them and gives them the run of the house. Paula is very upset when Sally's friend Jamie gets drunk and almost destroys their kitchen. The door of one cabinet has a hole in it, and a set of wicker shelves is ruined. It is difficult for Paula to comprehend these kids who seem to exploit Sally. They leave messages for her that are full of four-letter words. Paula goes to Mass on Sunday for "an hour of peace."

Sally is unsure whether to return to school, since she anticipates that her schedule will soon be changed. When she does not receive a return call from her guidance counselor, she feels angry. Mrs. Marx explains that, from the school's point of view, Sally is someone who has been truant and lazy. She has not handed in any work. Excuses come from both sides, the school's and Sally's. Sally receives inconsistent advice: Mr. West tells her he can change her schedule to suit her; Mrs. Marx says she doubts her schedule can be changed.

The next week Sally seems to be doing better. Uncle Robby had been visiting for the weekend and took her to the movies. Paula laments the move to this rural area away from her brother, who helped raise Sally and even taught her how to ride a bike when she was five. Those days seem irretrievable, indeed.

But Sally has been going to school for three hours per day now, taking Pottery, Gym, and History. She is anxious to fill out the rest of her program, which she will do through "Homebound Schooling." A math tutor visits two or three times a week and goes over several chapters. He reassures her that she will catch up.

After the Christmas holiday break, it seems that three steps forward lead to two steps backward. Sally skips two days of school and misses two history tests within a three-week period.

"I know I can do history. He will give me a fifty so I won't have a zero. Then I still have the next two marking periods. My mother is making mountains out of molehills," she announces. "My math and English are fine. I'm taking Spanish now, but I talked to Miss Masters about how it's not working."

The homebound Spanish teacher had stormed out a few days earlier stating that she was "not getting paid enough for this."

"I didn't understand the questions on the homework; I want to be taught, not babied." The Spanish teacher had accused her of wanting to be babied. Hearing this causes Paula to become very agitated, and she confesses to having argued a lot with Sally.

Jack has moved back to Paula's house. Paula agrees that Sally needs a friend. "She has no one, but I can't afford to feed him. They both eat like horses. The movies are eight dollars a person. I just can't do it. The car—they go cruising with no destination. It is fifteen to twenty dollars a week. I just can't do it." Sally says that Jack is adopted. For his first three years he was a foster child. After they adopted him and were no longer paid for keeping him, they decided they didn't want him anymore.

Weekend visits from extended family members seem, at times, to soften the tensions between mother and daughter. At other times, Sally feels that her mother and grandmother gang up on her. On one particular winter day Sally stayed home for her grandmother's visit and had a girlfriend spend the night. They baked brownies at 1:00 A.M., but that is okay. Paula remarked emphatically, "I'd rather they be here (home) than anywhere else." She makes a point of saying that the girlfriend is from the island.

There's a kind of desperation in Paula's caring, though. She wants Sally to set herself up for a good life, but she knows that once Sally reaches eighteen, she has no legal claim. For the moment, she tries to micromanage Sally's life. She polices with kindness and anxiety. "They (Sally and Jack) went to the store to pick up a few things. I gave them money and told them not to go over the amount. They did a good job." On another day, Sally and Jack collected cans from the beach. A garbage bag yields five dollars. "Good gas money," says Sally. On still another day Paula tells me Sally's self-esteem is in the basement. "I just don't

Class
Vulnerability

want her to make the same mistakes I did. I tell her that she was not a mistake. But I know she feels like one."

As a single parent who lives with and cares for Sally's dad, but defines it as "a job," Paula cannot help but send Sally mixed messages. Paula says Sally views her as not having accomplished anything in her life, which, Paula protests, is not true. Yet one wonders why Paula stays with him—"why," as Sally puts it, "she wants to change diapers."

The parallels between Jack, Sally's boyfriend, and Buck, Paula's "boyfriend" and Sally's father, are striking. Buck's "other," legal family does not want him; neither does Jack's island family want him. Paula is exploited by Buck and his disability. Sally is exploited by Jack's craziness and neediness, financial and psychological.

By midsemester Sally has missed eight days of school. Paula is cutting off any money and leaving her notes. It keeps Paula calmer. This is right before Sally's seventeenth birthday. Paula tells her mother and brother to keep the presents small. Paula is very angry at Sally, but she won't admit it. It does come out though, as Sally talks later about how miserable her birthday was, how Paula made shrimp for everyone and told Sally she should learn to eat shrimp even though she doesn't like it and had asked for clams on her birthday. Paula also protects Sally by lying about her school absences, but she says she will not lie anymore.

Because of her absenteeism, school officials want to put Sally back in school for the whole day. "Does she have to be a drug addict before they give her the attention?" Paula asks. "I was tempted to ask that at the last meeting with the principal," Paula confesses, "but I didn't want to make trouble."

Sally is very proud of the 100's, 92, and 94 on her math papers. She is now much more confident than ever. But she missed school during the whole last week of February, and Paula is very worried. She keeps telling Sally that she will never graduate from high school. This Sally resents deeply. "It's not what I need or want to hear."

Sally talks about her mother having no life, how young she is, and how she should go out. She worries that if her father dies, his legal family will go after the house unless Paula talks to a lawyer. She, Sally, admits that she does not want to be thinking about these issues, but that she is, nonetheless, worried about losing her home. She feels Paula is losing her sharpness. Paula admits to being very tired.

Sally states firmly that it would be disastrous for her to go to school for a whole day. She seems to function much better with home tutoring. She works well on her own and achieves at a high level. Yet she has so much noise in her head, distraction, insecurity, worry. She is more rational and analytical than Paula and has a clearer view of things than her mother. At the same time, she is in many ways a needy child, needy of love and confirmation. Few adults operate at her level of sophistication. Neither do many of the teachers in the school. She needs a combination of high intelligence and caring. Her math teacher seems, at least partially, to fit the bill.

The next week Paula has a conversation with Dr. Austin, Sally's pediatrician, asking if he'd be willing to sign a letter documenting the medical/psychological reasons why Sally needs to continue her homebound schooling. He does not want to sign it, claiming that "there are too many lawyers out there." He is afraid of getting sued for his lack of familiarity with Sally's situation since he has only seen her a few times in his office. The school principal and guidance counselors finally agree that homebound schooling would be best, but they need a letter from Sally's physician. At last Austin agrees to endorse the recommendations of the school.

At a meeting at the school the next week with the guidance counselor, Mrs. Marx, Paula, and Sally, in the principal's office, the principal acts like a real bureaucrat. He tries to be helpful but states clearly that his job is to have students come to school. He does agree, however, to maintain Sally's math and English as homebound schooling and to contact Dr. Austin.

Sally looks despondent; she's dressed in black, with lots of dark eye makeup. She refuses to make eye contact with anybody. She answers questions in short, monosyllabic responses. It's clear she just wants to get out of there as soon as possible.

Suddenly Jack starts stalking Sally. After he battered her car and came at her with a two-by-four, she told him to get out of her house. She confesses that she does not feel safe anywhere, especially at school and at home. Paula contacts the police, both on the island and in Breckenridge. She realizes that Jack is still controlling Sally's life and understands that counseling for victims of stalkers is in order. For Sally, the car battering is the final blow. She cannot go back to him. She immediately finds a new boyfriend, who appears to be much more stable and sensitive to her needs. Jack has finally exited from her life. She continues to do her math and English at home but does not attend school. Paula is going for counseling, and the household appears to be calmer, at least for the time being.

EPILOGUE

By the end of the year, Sally has discontinued the homebound schooling and has decided to take the GED exam. She wonders whether this will jeopardize her college chances. Her plan is now to get her GED, attend the local community college, and then transfer to a state university.

She passes the GED exam easily and is now working as a bank teller, a job she likes and is good at. She has always been very organized, and she is good in math. In June, when her high school class is graduating, she asks Paula for a graduation party. Paula refuses, and Sally is angry; she talks about being showered with material things but never being told she is doing a good job. She talks about getting her own apartment, how she can't bear the constant criticism and intense scrutiny, but she feels a strong responsibility for her parents and still wants their approval. She realizes that getting a GED was more difficult than going through school, but she also knows that it doesn't carry the same rights and privileges, the same legal claim.

Epilogue

SHOOBIES GO HOME

I hate their noise and their bratty children.
They let them scream like gibbons in the zoo.

They think they own my space, my ocean, my bay, my island that
*   I've loved from childhood.*

Their cars pierce the silence of my peace
My dog barks when they tease her
She understands
They play, intensely—tennis racquets, jet skis that sound like
*   mosquitoes buzzing in your ear at night, sail boats—*
but ignorantly.
Slam! goes the boat's bow.
The mast hangs on the bulkhead.
Storms come up quickly.

"Hey! Where you going?" yells an anxious child, afraid his white
*   tennis skirted mother will abandon him yet again.*

The gravel driveway crunches. My dog barks again.
But this mom's just moving her car from one side of the driveway
*   to the other—too fast, of course.*

They make me want to curl up and hibernate for the summer.
I'll come out after labor day.

Benj, 14, who cleans on his mother's crew, flunked two subjects at
*   the local high school.*
It's a prison.
He says shoobies have no respect.
He's wise.
They don't.

I read once that in Mexico they call certain people "*arribistas,*"
or climbers, from the word *arriba,* meaning above or high up.
Arribistas are people who are trying to reach the top of the ladder. It's not always clear exactly what kind of ladder they are
climbing or exactly when they know they have reached the top,
but one thing is for certain: *arribistas* are constantly striving to
move up.

They have things, many things: motor boats, outdoor speakers
blasting Barbra Streisand, jet skis, BMWs and SUVs, swimming
pools, manicured landscaping, trips to Europe and around the
world. Don't they know that boom boxes have been banned in
New York's Central Park? They do know they have ambitions,
often blind ambitions, for money, power, careers. Their sons
and brothers come speeding in on the jet ski—maybe it's a
waverunner, I don't know. They don't know that there are rules
about wake, the waves motor boats create when they are going
fast. Wake can damage bulkheads and boats that are docked.
Thus, the rule that "no wake" be made anywhere near shore.
Slow is the watchword. But they don't care if my wooden row-
boat bangs against the dock and is smashed to splinters. They
don't even notice the people swimming near shore. They also
don't know that one big storm could wipe away everything, including their bonsai trees and fancy perennial gardens. You see,
they are "shoobies," newcomers, wealthy newcomers, who live
here only in summer. In the forties and fifties, we locals used
the term "shoobies" to talk about the day trippers who would

come to the beach and bring their lunches in shoe boxes. We loved it when the shoobies went home for the winter.

One family claims they can't get their huge motorboat around a sailboat that's kept out on an open mooring. It's a small sailboat at that—only nineteen feet. Anyone who knows how fiercely the winds can whip across the bay puts boats out on moorings to swing freely. That way, they don't hit up against wooden docks or pilings. Go to the big harbors in Maine and Massachusetts and you'll see thousands of boats on open moorings. There's plenty of room to steer around that lone sailboat, if you know how to navigate. But maybe they feel they are entitled to the whole bay, unobstructed. Is it the view they are worried about? Is it private property? The mother of the family became upset that a neighbor was tying a line from his small kayak to her piling on the east side of her empty boat slip. She had no idea that boat lines share pilings.

Fathers push around innocent three-year-olds, literally and figuratively. They talk abusively in very loud tones so that everyone can hear. The children cower; they're scared. The water in their swimming pool carries sound. What good is an expensive summer house when it destroys a child's self-esteem? Why anyone would want a tiny dunking pool next to the expansive bay is beyond me. Two strokes and you're at the other end, that is, if you don't first bang your head against the wall. Their children screech as they play in those swimming pools, parents looking on with their martinis and their minted iced tea, oblivious to the idea that I might want to study and think, or that I might need to sleep after working all night.

Their house is named "Bay Dream." It seems odd to me to give a house a name, but they seem to be fixed on names for everything. Is it that they want to leave a legacy? Maybe they live in a perpetual dream, an unreal world unto itself? But it causes me nightmares. There's a grandmother and grandfather, in their sixties, I'd say. They each have grown children from their first marriages and lots of grandchildren. They smile a lot, but they don't seem to mean it. It is as though they think they are supposed to smile, just like they are supposed to have big boats and big,

The Teacup Ministry and Other Stories

expensive cars. Money rules them. Perhaps it's their business mentality. I wonder what it's like building elevators, elevators for large buildings—supervising factories in several cities. What a responsibility, to make sure that people don't get stuck on the thirty-second floor. People do, after all, need elevators.

We grew up on this island—through the storms, hurricanes, and floods. In summer we played freely in the ocean, built sand castles, played ball. In winter we went to school. Mom was a nurse then. My father was a construction worker all his life—that is, until he had a paralyzing stroke. He can't move his whole left side. He copes with it marvelously, though. He's precious. His sense of humor alone would be material for several stand-up comics to have successful careers. We—that is, my sister, brother, and I—take turns caring for him during the day.

My sister's a nurse and my brother's a cop, with a few small businesses on the side. He just started a linen service, which seems to be growing. She has to drive fifty miles south to work every day at the hospital. She's used to it by now.

My father built many of the houses on our street. They're well built, so sturdy that people have trouble figuring out how to take them apart for rehab.

My mom has him at night. It's a privilege. He's so appreciative. On sunny days we take him to that same beach of our childhood in a special wheelchair with huge plastic wheels. The township provides them for its citizens with disabilities free of charge. People stare at us because of this very unusual-looking wheelchair, but we don't care. Sometimes we bring a thermos of Manhattans, his very favorite drink. Other days I take him to the diner, where he always sees old friends and eats his favorite foods, macaroni and cheese or biscuits and gravy. Just the joy of seeing my father so happy makes me feel that the world is right. My sister and I both take Wednesdays off from work so we can do things together. If my sister needs to work, I just take a peaceful day for reading at the beach, or, more likely, for cleaning our house.

In summer I work at the seafood house down the road. I really like it. The owners are wonderful to me, although I can't see why people come to eat there in droves. It's rustic. The place isn't air conditioned; so if the customers are sweating, imagine what it is like for the servers—a real upper-body workout it is carrying those heavy trays. But it's a welcome relief from the pressures of graduate school in the winter. I make a lot of money in tips, enough to get me through until the next summer.

In winter, I must drive two hours north to attend classes in geriatric social work. There's such a need. The elderly have so much to teach us. If I'm lucky, when I graduate, I'll get a job at the social service center on the island. That way I can be near Dad. In winter I scrounge for jobs: dog-sitting and taking care of an elderly woman is about the extent of it. Balancing school and home is difficult, but not in the ways people usually think of it. Last year I could have taken a full-time course load, but it would have meant rushing through the reading and feeling pressured all the time with school. I wouldn't be able to enjoy my time with Dad.

A lot of people think that school should always come first. Study, study, study—no life, no family, especially not the family of your parents. Mothers with small children are cut some slack, even fathers these days can be understood as parents. But I have responsibility for parents, Dad especially. People don't understand how much home means to me and my sister, how important Mom and Dad are to us. They expect that because I attend the university, I will forget my parents or only go visit them on holidays. I lived in the city for a while, for all of undergraduate school, in fact. I missed the ocean, but even more I missed my family, the little, everyday insignificant things, like hearing Dad laugh, seeing his joy in his friends, being around his upbeat spirit in the face of such serious disability.

Unfortunately, my boyfriend did not understand any of this— the fact that I would even have been willing to give up my career and take a lesser job. He did not want to move out of the city. I chose my family over him and the city. You don't appreciate where you live until you have been somewhere else.

Shoobies are really ruining the world, aren't they? They seem to have misplaced values, somehow. What is important to them is not important to me.

These stories are about the experiences and expressions of class in everyday life: the small things that give people a sense of belonging in certain places, with certain people, at certain times are the essence of class culture. I want to emphasize the interpretive qualities of these stories as well as their yarn-like nature. As they unravel, they are meant to be retold in transformed ways to fit other circumstances, other people, and other places. Class culture is often fragmented or hidden, but it figures in subtle but important ways in all people's lives—people of different ethnicities and races, rich and poor, young and old, men and women. Class experiences are cultural processes that bring people of similar and different life circumstances together and split them apart. These class interactions, in turn, transform the experiences and meanings of class itself.

The everyday and changing manifestations of class culture and local knowledge portrayed in these stories reveal resiliency, imagination, and sharp wit and humor, as well as forms of discrimination, vulnerability, and real danger. The ways in which people cross class boundaries and the consequences of those crossings are the themes of Part I. Class creativity—talents and personalized forms of expression—artifacts, design, humor, clever strategizing are the themes of Part II. The stories about class vulnerability and danger in Part III are designed to counter stereotypes and generalizations about violence, incest, and abuse. The themes of the three sections are overlapping, however, and one could easily make arguments for placing individual stories in one part rather than another.

The nuances of class culture and local knowledge are often so subtle that they are missed by even the most astute observers. The many shadings of class discrimination resemble the more blatant forms of gender, race, and ethnic discrimination throughout the world, but class discrimination is still unstudied and acceptable, even, and often especially, in the most enlightened of circles, academia included. The stories here are about lines—boundary lines—between people of different life situations and life chances, that is, classes. Some of these lines are clear—sharp, in fact. Some are not. Some are drawn and some not. The cultural constructions of boundaries and the ways in which class boundaries define and create identities and senses of self are central elements in this project.[1]

Attachment to place creates contexts in which class spaces can be violated, invaded, and even harmed. The subtle boundaries between public and private space, common or community space, and class space within these localities are treated in many of the stories. Locality itself is a complicated and problematic concept. It both defines and is defined by class.

Class has always been a traditional[2] but abstract topic in the social sciences.[3] It has been the subject of theories that debate its character, its composition, and its structure.[4] It is a concept that has been discussed, dissected, and debated, but rarely understood in tangible, gut-level ways.[5]

To real people, the experiences of class are rooted in everyday life. Class experiences, though, are not ordinarily labeled as such. They are taken for granted as practices not worthy of attention precisely because they are ordinary, day-to-day routines. As global forces propel people of different classes and cultures together in new, and often uncomfortable, contexts, the experiences of class change and problematize the nature of class itself. Class issues become mixed and confused, often with issues of gender, race, and ethnicity. The boundaries of class may become fluid and permeable, but compelling nonetheless.

This project is a synthesis and new interpretation of years of anthropological research in U.S. working-class communities, rural and urban.[6] Much of this research has focused on livelihood—strategies that are regionally situated, labor intensive, and resistant to dependence upon conventional, mainstream systems of knowledge and power, both economic and political.[7] I had spent years thinking about creativity in the practical, economic sense—that is, in terms of the strategies for survival at the margins of a deindustrializing nation-state. But creativity must be thought about holistically if we are to understand the resiliency of people in global cultures. By this I mean that creativity is part of all aspects of everyday life, from the fashioning of artifacts that are used as gifts to the coping strategies at City Hall. Ordinary people develop and express creative talents in a multitude of hidden, often private, but sometimes public, ways.

If my past work has foregrounded community and structure by seeing people as engaging in practices that grow out of and perpetuate membership in class culture and community, the focus here is the reverse. People and practices are in the foreground, with community and culture as background. Here I am interested in the impact of changing structure (class structure, community structure, family structure) on a person's sense of agency (self). The things I learned in the course of my work and my life as an anthropologist—the things that seemed to stick in my mind, but that never made it out of my field notes into print—are central elements in this book precisely because they are elements of class culture that few people write about. The short story format makes it possible to deal with complicated issues in an accessible and compact style.

This book contributes to the rethinking of class by seeing power in everyday life and in the systems of relationships and differences that culture and economy jointly create. If, as Foucault[8] would have it, power is an element of all social relations and contexts, then we need to elaborate this important point and build on it by showing how local contextualized power relations play out. These need to be analyzed as contributing to new ways of thinking about class, for class is always present in social relationships. In increasingly global contexts, class can override or, at the very least, undermine differences of gender, race, ethnicity, and nationality.

Notes

PROLOGUE TO PART II

1. Barbara Kirshenblatt-Gimblett, in an essay entitled "Objects of Ethnography," has the following to say about what she calls "ethnographic artifacts": "Ethnographic artifacts are objects of ethnography. They are artifacts created by ethnographers. Objects become ethnographic by virtue of being defined, segmented, detached, and carried away by ethnographers." In Ivan Karp and Steven D. Lavine, *Exhibiting Cultures* (Washington, D.C.: Smithsonian, 1991), p. 387.

AFTERWORD

1. In anthropology and history see the work of Louise Lamphere, Hill Gates, Paul Willis, and Michael Taussig. I am certainly writing in the tradition of Marxist analysis—theory, historiography, ethnography, inspired particularly by E. P. Thompson, Eric Hobsbawm (particularly his book *Bandits*), and Raymond Williams. See also Erving Goffman, *The Presentation of Self in Everyday Life* (Garden City, N.J.: Doubleday, 1959), and Michel de Certau, *The Practice of Everyday Life* (Berkeley: University of California Press, 1984).

2. See the classic and still often cited work by E. P. Thompson, *The Making of the English Working Class*. More recent work includes Ira Katznelson and Aristide R. Zolberg, eds., *Working Class Formation: Nineteenth-Century Pattern in Western Europe and the United States* (Princeton, N.J.: Princeton University Press, 1998); and Patrick Joyce, *Visions of the People: Industrial England and the Question of Class* (Cambridge: Cambridge University Press, 1991).

3. Patrick Joyce talks about the concept of class coming "under increasing scrutiny as a means of explaining both the present and the past." He goes on to say that the questioning of class in the context of postindustrial society and a globalized economy must address changes in the nature and significance of work, which in turn have "considerable effect on people's sense of collective and personal identity." Joyce also points out that "in a time when 'movement,' or 'identity' politics such as the politics of gender and ethnic groups is so important, the identity that had not been registered in this 'identity' politics is that of class" (Patrick Joyce, Introduction, in Joyce, ed., *Class* [Oxford: Oxford University Press, 1995], pp. 3–4).

4. Most discussions of class are rather abstract and removed from everyday life experience even though they may assert the importance of such experience; see Anthony Giddens, *The Class Structure of Advanced Societies* (London: Hutchinson, 1973); as well as E. O. Wright, et al., *The Debate on Classes* (New York: Verso, 1989), and his book *Class Counts: Comparative Studies in Class Analysis* (Cambridge: Cambridge University Press, 1996).

Even those discussions that argue for examining class more concretely do not do so in any detail. See Sonya O. Rose, "Resuscitating Class," in *Social Science History* 22.1 (Spring 1998): 19–27, and also Evelyn Nakano Glenn, "Gender, Race and Class: Bridging the Language-Structure Divide," *Social Science History* 22.1 (Spring 1998): 29–38.

An interesting recent book is John R. Hall, ed., *Reworking Class* (New York: Cornell University Press, 1998); see especially Hall's introduction, "The Reworking of Class Analysis," and articles by Margaret Somers, Sonya Rose, and John Walton.

5. For an exception, albeit outside of the social sciences, see *Women's Studies Quarterly* 23, nos. 1 and 2 (Spring/Summer 1995), which is devoted to working class studies.

6. My *Practicing Community* (Austin: University of Texas Press, 1998) is the result of long-term, ongoing research and advocacy in Cincinnati's East End.

7. *The Livelihood of Kin* (Austin: University of Texas Press, 1990).

8. See Michel Foucault, *Power/Knowledge: Selected Interviews and Other Writings, 1972–1977,* edited by Colin Gordon, translated by Colin Gordon et al. (New York: Pantheon Books, 1980).

Printed and bound by CPI Group (UK) Ltd, Croydon, CR0 4YY

13/04/2025

14656493-0004